Moving Forward, Courageously

Courageously

*Unleash Your Inner Strength, Embrace Change,
and Conquer Life's Challenges with Confidence*

Ellard "Coach Ell" Thomas

To my "strong whys" – Kimberly and Ellard. Your courage gives me the strength to continue onward and upward despite adverse circumstances and uncertainty.

Contents

Why This Book? i

Preface... iii

Chapter 1: The Elements 1

Chapter 2: Choose 11

Chapter 3: Oppose Failure 44

Chapter 4: Use the Power of Negative Emotions for Positive Action.. 71

Chapter 5: Reject Doubt 83

Chapter 6: Acknowledge Your Strong Whys......................... 112

Chapter 7: Get Back Up Again 127

Chapter 8: Evolve into Your True Self................................. 143

Chapter 9: Mastering the Art of Living Courageously........... 159

References 169

Why This Book?

Finding happiness is often considered the ultimate goal in life. Happiness is a universal aspiration, whether it is tied to financial success, the warmth of love, or the satisfaction of personal achievements. Regrettably, unforeseen challenges and the painful sting of loss have stood in your way, preventing you from fully realizing this quest for happiness. But today, we declare an end to this struggle as you embark on a new journey toward a more joyful and fulfilling existence.

Thomas Jefferson, a prominent figure in the drafting of the Declaration of Independence, emphasized the idea that every individual possesses unalienable rights to "life, liberty, and the pursuit of happiness." One might wonder why he didn't simply use the word "happiness" instead of including the word "pursuit."

Happiness is a concept that varies greatly from person to person. For some, it's synonymous with financial independence, while for others, it's rooted in love, and there are those who associate it with wealth or good health. Regardless of how one defines it, happiness is something everyone deserves, but it doesn't come to you on a silver platter. You must fight against the currents of destitution and winds of adversity to obtain it.

During a drive around Seattle, my good friend Alex asked me a thought-provoking question. "Ellard," she said, "have you ever felt like you were walking in a dark tunnel, and no matter how long you walked, there was no sign of light?"

Her eyes welled up with tears as the pain from a recent breakup etched her face with sadness.

"Yes, I did," I answered, as I thought about my own struggles.

"What did you do?" she asked.

"I kept moving forward, courageously..."

In the face of pain and suffering, it's essential to summon your inner courage and persevere, even when you're tempted to surrender or give up. Always keep in mind that the life you long for is waiting on the other side. By embracing the principles outlined here, you will not only build the confidence and strength needed to conquer feelings of depression, discouragement, and hopelessness but also make significant strides in both your personal and professional life. Get ready to feel exhilarated because you are on the brink of transforming your life for the better.

Preface

Discovering the Secrets

I found life to be cold and callous—a mockery of giving. Whenever I thought I had achieved happiness, life ripped it from my grasp and handed me hopelessness and misery in return. Determined to live a fulfilling life, I pursued happiness even harder. Still, no matter how hard I worked for it, happiness appeared dimly in the far distance, as if it were beyond my reach. It took losing every dollar I had in an investment opportunity to become enlightened by the secrets to restoring happiness and success in my life.

I had been working as a national accounts manager for a local engineering firm when the entrepreneurial bug bit me. Even though I exceeded each sales goal, the company had no advancement opportunities available for me. Driven to reach financial independence, I entertained the thought of pursuing another avenue.

Sitting at my desk, I peered out the window, thinking about my recent string of losses. A month prior, I had lost my home in a painful divorce, forcing me to rent an apartment in an undesirable part of town. A week later, my car, a graduation gift from my sister, was stolen. I felt the world crumbling around me. Making money quickly had become my only focus.

My phone rang and woke me from my trance. It was my good friend Troy, a successful mortgage broker.

"Ellard..." he said.

"What is it, Troy?" I sighed.

"Business is booming. My phones are ringing off the hook! This is too much for one person to handle. Why don't we team up so you can make the type of money you deserve?"

"Really?" I asked, wondering if this was the opportunity I had prayed for.

"Would I ever steer you wrong?" he asked in a fatherly manner.

"Yes!"

"For real?" he questioned, sounding wounded. "Are you still holding a grudge against me?"

Five years prior to his phone call, I had joined Troy in a multi-level marketing company and realized that, even though I believed in the business model, it wasn't what I really wanted to do.

"No," I said and laughed. "That's in the past!"

"So, are you in?" he asked.

"I suppose, Troy. Give me two weeks."

"Sounds good! I can't wait to have you aboard."

Shortly after our conversation, I peered through the window once again, taking a deep breath. *Was I ready to leave a company that provided me with health benefits, job security, 401K contributions, and a steady paycheck*? Realizing that I wanted more for my life, I walked down the aisle of the boisterous sales floor and stood at the vice president of sales' office door.

"May I speak with you, Jeff?" I asked.

"Mr. Thomas," he smiled. "To what do I owe this pleasure..."

Jeff spent an hour trying to get me to change my mind; I didn't. Losing the get-Ellard-to-stay battle, he finally accepted my two weeks' notice.

My Hell on Earth

> *"If you're going through hell, keep going."*
>
> -*Winston Churchill*

Shortly after partnering with Troy, a dramatic shift unfolded in the once-thriving finance market. The business flow abruptly came to a halt as banks tightened their lending criteria, leaving homeowners to bear the brunt. Despite thoughts of reverting to my former employer spreading like wildfire, the fear of failure and my pride prevented me from taking a step backward. Instead, I gritted my teeth and committed a substantial portion of my savings to salvage the struggling business.

As the market conditions deteriorated, we found ourselves drowning in debt, facing the harsh reality that we were on the verge of bankruptcy. A sense of despair took hold of my heart. The loan applications that lenders had initially approved and scheduled to fund were abruptly canceled, with many businesses folding. The promises of lucrative commission checks vanished into thin air, taking my happiness with them. With only a meager few hundred dollars left in my emergency fund, I realized that I had to weather this storm, and something needed to change – and fast.

Meeting Coach

"Be wise in the way you act toward outsiders; make the most of every opportunity."

-Colossians 4:5 (NIV)

During one of our morning drives, while we were strategizing how to overcome the readjusting mortgage market, Troy pulled into the parking lot of a massive brick building.

"Why are we here?" I asked, a bit upset and reluctant to get out of the car. "I thought we were going to put together an action plan."

"I need to see Coach," he said.

"Who's Coach?" I grunted.

"Coach is an old businessman with whom I developed a business relationship a few years ago," he smirked. "He would send me clients, and I would do the same for him. Besides, he told me that if I ever needed anything, I could come and see him. I spoke with him the other day and requested a favor. I'm here to collect on it."

"Whatever!" I snarled.

Getting out of the car, we entered through the cherrywood door, stood in the lobby, and greeted the receptionist.

"Is Coach here?" Troy asked the receptionist.

"I'll call and check," she said.

We waited a moment.

"He's in his office," the receptionist smiled as she hung up the phone.

"Thank you," Troy grinned.

"Ellard," he turned to me, "I'll be back."

"Where are you going?" I asked as frustration took a stronger hold of me.

"Just wait here."

I sat on the lobby couch and thumbed through a couple of business magazines. Troy returned 20 minutes later, smirking. He pulled me into a nearby office.

"I'd like to ask you a question," he said.

"What?" I asked.

He placed his hands on my shoulders and stared into my eyes.

"Would you entertain an opportunity if it could help you recoup your money?" he asked.

"Of course, Troy!" I answered. "What are you thinking?"

"Since the lending industry isn't doing so well," Troy continued, "I thought you'd like to learn the commercial real estate business and hopefully earn back everything you invested with me."

"How is that possible?" I squinted.

"Coach is a multimillionaire who's looking to teach his business techniques to someone he can trust. I told him a lot about you, and he wants to speak with you."

"Very well," I sighed.

A stern-faced old man with well-groomed silver hair and a white beard entered the office, interrupting our conversation.

"Coach," Troy smiled, "this is my friend, Ellard."

Coach gave me a look-over.

"How are you doing?" he asked.

"I'm well," I said, shaking the gentleman's aged but strong hand.

"Troy," Coach said. "Leave me and E-lord."

Coach already had insulted me by mispronouncing my name. Troy exited the office. Coach and I sat at his table.

"Troy tells me you're interested in learning the commercial real estate business," Coach started. "Is this correct?"

"Yes," I answered.

"Is it only about money?" Coach inquired, staring at me.

"Pretty much," I replied. "I lost everything I owned and need to do whatever I can to recover from my losses."

Coach stroked his beard and gazed out the window. Moments of silence stood between us.

"If I take you on as a student, I need you to do me one favor," he stated.

"Anything," I answered, thinking how this opportunity could help me out of my financial rut.

Coach grinned.

"Don't quit," he chuckled. "This business isn't easy. But if you stay at it, you'll encounter the 'magic' that will help you achieve your financial goals!"

"Okay," I answered, hiding my excitement.

"Good," Coach said with a wince and got to his feet. "I hope that you're a worthwhile risk."

"Me too," I said.

"Meet me here tomorrow," he replied. "There's much for us to do."

I rose to my feet and shook Coach's hand. He escorted me to the front door.

"Thank you for this opportunity," I said with a smile. "I won't let you down. By the way, what time should I be here?" I asked, standing at the door.

"Early," Coach answered. "We start our mornings early!"

I left the building, and Troy waved me over to the car.

"How was it?" he smiled, giddily.

"It was okay," I said as I hopped in the car.

"Okay?" Troy asked, surprised. "If everything goes well, you'll be working with a millionaire!"

I wasn't impressed by Coach's massive building, nor did I care about his financial status. I only cared about bringing an end to my monetary woes.

The Lesson

"Things turn out best for those who make the best of the way things turn out."

Coach had a peculiar way of training me in the commercial real estate business. I expected that he would sit me down and devise a strategy or introduce me to his business associates, as a true mentor would. I was not even close. Rather than show me the ropes (as I had hoped), he hired me as the office help, paying me less than minimum wage. Each day for a month, my job was to answer the phones, "Go there...," "Get this...," "Copy these...," and "Deliver this...." I cringed with each request, wondering if he would ever reveal his real estate secrets to me.

The Secrets Revealed

"An idea, to be suggestive, must come to the individual with the force of revelation."

-*William James*

I was ecstatic when I received my real estate license. I knew for sure that Coach would teach me the business. Again, he disappointed me. Without teaching me one skill, Coach gave me some "training" leads and pushed this little lamb into a world of vicious wolves. Prospective clients dropped me for more seasoned professionals. Agents, who represented properties where I brought the few trusting clients I had, caught a whiff of the new blood and found ways to cut me out of the deals. I did everything I could to pull myself up by the bootstraps. Unfortunately, my exhaustive efforts ended with a dwindling bank account and sorrow. I wanted to quit. I wanted to yell. I wanted to call Troy and give him a piece of my mind. Then something strange happened. One evening, as I sat at my computer, on the brink of a nervous breakdown, I finally discovered the "magic" that Coach had mentioned during our first meeting. Enlightened, I leaned back and started laughing.

"Coach, you ass," I said, shaking my head, replaying every failed meeting and broken deal. "You almost made me give up."

Coach's lack of direction and odd treatment was not only his way of teaching me a lesson but a metaphor for life. Life makes us undergo numerous pains, defeats, and losses before it reveals the methods by which happiness and success are achieved and restored. It purposely forces us to look within ourselves for the innate power that pushes us to overcome all our anguish, hurt, and pain. This revelation gave me a new perspective on my current situation and my life. Coach didn't achieve riches and the lifestyle I wanted because he was better than me. No, he had effectively and repeatedly used the "magic" or secrets that I went on to discover. From that moment on, I became intensely determined to succeed. I became obsessed with regaining my financial stability. Before every deal, I would visualize thousands of dollars filling my bank account. Removed from worry and financial distress, I changed how I saw Coach's training leads. They were opportunities for me to build the confidence and creative thinking skills necessary to succeed in a dog-eat-dog industry. My victimized mindset was replaced with the mindset of a champion. Within one year, I earned Coach's respect and (his real estate tricks), recouped all my losses, and started my own consulting company. All this was done by implementing the secrets of moving forward courageously.

Chapter 1
The Elements

"Don't dwell on what went wrong!

Instead, focus on what to do next.

Spend your energies on moving forward toward finding the answer!"

-Denis Waitley

When confronted with despair, uncertainty, and sorrow arising from loss or any other emotionally or mentally debilitating challenge, it's common for individuals to abandon their dreams and halt their pursuit of goals. Motivation dwindles, productivity declines, and life loses its vibrancy, becoming mundane and repetitive.

The pathway to conquering life's obstacles, which hinder our success and happiness, lies in moving forward with courage. Forward motion is vital for life's progression. Just as children, once born, can never return to the womb but must journey through the stages of development and eventually come to terms with nature at life's end, so too must we continue moving forward. Time, like the passing of day and night, cannot be reversed, and the actions tied to its passing cannot be undone. Embracing this natural principle, you should apply it to your own life.

For countless individuals, progressing forward presents a huge challenge. Heartbreaks, financial struggles, health setbacks, and the grief of losing loved ones can trigger overwhelming emotional turmoil. In response, we often find ourselves paralyzed, unable to move forward. In moments of anguish, tears flow, and despair echoes in cries of "I can't endure this" or "I can't carry on." Blinded by the dense fog of sorrow, we fail to perceive the glimmer of happiness awaiting us. Instead, we're consumed by the unanswerable query: "Why is this happening to me?"

As we find ourselves buried beneath the wreckage of unfortunate events, thoughts of happiness often fade into the background. Yet, before succumbing to despair, we must acknowledge a crucial truth: Time stops for no one. Relentlessly, it marches on, leaving us behind and aging us despite our reluctance to move forward. Every moment spent mired in fear, bitterness, disbelief, or sorrow only heightens our vulnerability to failure, prolonged unhappiness, and a host of other undesirable consequences. Thus, to propel ourselves forward, we need only tap into the inherent strength we possess: courage.

The Power of Courage

"Each time we face our fear, we gain strength, courage, and confidence in the doing."

-Anonymous

Courage has proven to be a strong ally for countless individuals, enabling them to confront daunting challenges, recover from setbacks, and conquer formidable obstacles. My own appreciation for this invaluable trait deepened significantly during my time as a young Marine Corps recruit when I found myself confronted with an exceptionally demanding task.

My platoon marched from the barracks to the "stairway to heaven," a 30-foot, 90-degree ladder appearing to breach the sky.

"Who out here is afraid of heights?" my drill instructor asked.

My hand shot up foolishly in the air.

"Very well," he continued, "come here, Thomas."

"Sir, yes, sir!"

I marched over to the drill instructor and stood before him in the position of attention.

"You see that ammo can at the top?" he said, pointing to the clouds.

"Yes, sir!"

"Bring it to me!"

Huh? I questioned in my mind. *Climb that*? *Didn't I say I was afraid of heights*? I could fall easily through the gaps between each step.

"I ain't got all day, Thomas!" My drill instructor barked. "Hurry the hell up!"

Okay, I can do this, I told myself. *I'm on the first step, yippee*! I looked up. *Lord, have mercy on me. Don't let me fall*. My fellow recruits watched fretfully as I took another step. Nearly losing my footing, I grabbed the pole in panic, too afraid to keep climbing.

"I'm waiting, Thomas!" my drill instructor hollered.

I inhaled deeply and looked up. *So far to go.* Following one reach and pull after the other, I finally reached the top. "It's beautiful up here," I whispered, straddling the bar for dear life.

I had the ammo can, but now what? I had two hands coming up but only one available to descend. A two-inch mat at the base of the stairway waited to catch me. It was not a thought I wished to entertain.

Very slowly, I negotiated each step as I descended the ladder, praying not to fall.

Following a few close calls, I made it to the ground safely, ammunition can in hand. I faced my drill instructor with my heart racing.

"Very good," he said. "Now put my damn ammo can back where you got it! What the hell, Thomas?"

I stared at my drill instructor. *Do it again? Heck! Why send me up there in the first place if he didn't want it?* I sighed and then faced the difficult task before me. Ammo can securely under my left arm, I climbed once again toward the heavens, concentrating, with all my focus on succeeding. *Mission completed!*

Following hours of torturous training, the platoon and I marched back to the barracks. As everyone settled in and prepared for class, I found my drill instructor alone in his office.

"Permission to enter, sir?" I asked.

"What is it, Thomas?" He stared coldly at me.

"Sir," I said, "why did you call on me to be the first to climb the stairway?"

He looked around to ensure that no one was standing behind me.

"You were the first one to bravely admit his lack of courage," he said with a smirk. "I needed you to be an example to the rest of the platoon. Most people rarely face their inner obstacles squarely. To you, a job well done!"

"Thank you," I said with a smile.

Two recruits suddenly approached me from behind.

"Now drop and give me sixty for smiling Thomas!" he yelled.

"What do you think this is, a damn comedy show?"

I dropped to the floor, counting out my pushups. "Honor, courage, commitment...one..."

Life is a series of ups and downs. Throughout our lives, we'll experience emotional highs and emotional lows. The courage necessary to ascend the ladder of happiness and success is the same courage we must use to face the challenges and losses responsible for our emotional descents.

Courage

"The key to change...is to let go of fear!"

-Rosanne Cash

Many dictionaries define courage as bravery, strength, fortitude, and will. For the sake of argument, courage is **"the quality of mind or spirit** that enables a person to face difficulty, danger, and pain." This is the power that helps you to move forward through the path of uncertainty and unknown circumstances toward achieving the life you desire. It is the energizing catalyst that promotes change—change in our attitudes, perceptions of the obstacles we face, and our current emotional and living conditions. It helps us to keep moving forward through the ashes and ruins of anguish, sorrow, heartache, sickness, and anything else that obstructs our vision of the life we ultimately desire. The story that follows stands as a compelling testament to the true embodiment of courage, demonstrating its profound impact and inspirational potential.

~ Mrs. Johnson drives up to her house after a mother-and-daughter day at the local market. She releases her four-year-old from the car seat and lets her play with her new ball in the yard.

Retrieving the groceries from the car, Mrs. Johnson notices that her daughter is not in the yard. She looks around. Terrified, she sees her daughter following her ball into the middle of the street as a speeding pickup truck flies around the corner.

Overcome with the fear of losing her daughter, the loving mother drops her groceries and sprints insanely to the child. With only moments to spare, she leaps through the air, grabs her daughter, and rolls to a stop. Elbows bleeding and head bruised, she looks at her daughter, inspecting her for injuries. The little child smiles as if her life had never been in jeopardy.

When fortified by courage, our potential knows few bounds. Regrettably, for many of us, it often takes dire circumstances or the imminent threat of loss to muster the strength to overcome formidable challenges. So why is it that we find it difficult to summon courage when it comes to enhancing or reclaiming our lives? Fear is usually the culprit.

Fear—My Friend or Foe?

"Always do what you are afraid to do."

- *Ralph Waldo Emerson*

Napoleon Hill, perhaps one of the most recognized inspirational figures in history and the author of many inspiring books, such as *The Laws of Success* and the multi-million selling *Think and Grow Rich*, implies that fear is the reason we fail to progress in every area of our lives.

"The majority of people, if asked what they fear most, would reply, 'I fear nothing.' The reply would be inaccurate, because few people realize that they are bound, handicapped, whipped spiritually and mentally through some form of fear."

Fear operates as a relentless antagonist, a bigmouthed bully that threatens to strip away our hopes of happiness and shatter our aspirations for joy. Its insidious whispers aim to convince us that rebuilding and revitalizing our lives are futile endeavors. Once we succumb to this deceit, we find ourselves adrift like grains of sand at the mercy of the ocean's currents.

In my own experience, a childhood adversary named Rowan provided a powerful lesson in confronting fear head-on.

~ Every morning before school, I would play basketball outside with my friends on our school's outdoor court. Each morning, Rowan, a skateboard-riding, bushy, redheaded boy whose favorite pastime was shoving and beating up on the other kids, would start trouble. He'd take the littler boys' lunch money, pull the girls' hair, and push other boys to the ground who didn't have money. If he didn't bother me, I paid him no attention. Well, my turn finally had come.

As I played with my friends in the gym, Rowan skated over to me.

"Ellard!" he yelled as he skated toward me.

"What?" I replied nervously.

"Today, I want you to clean my shoes!"

"Yeah, right!" I whispered.

Rowan hopped off his skateboard and kicked me in the butt. I did nothing, too afraid. He laughed and kicked me again. The other kids laughed and pointed at me. Paralysis set in. My heart thumped faster. Standing amid chuckles and giggles, I walked away to avoid further humiliation and punishment.

"Yeah, you better run, coward!" Rowan yelled as I fought back my tears.

For the next few weeks, I became Rowan's favorite target. The kids' laughter finally got to me and brought me to my wit's end, but I didn't know what to do.

Upon arriving home one day, I decided that I didn't want to be Rowan's spectacle. I stormed into the house.

"Mom," I shouted, tears filling my eyes, "where are you?"

"In the kitchen, Ellard."

"Mom," I said as I entered the kitchen, "can I talk to you?"

"What, son?" she responded, cutting up potatoes for dinner.

"There's this kid at school who keeps kicking me," I said softly.

My mother stopped cutting and looked directly at me.

"Why?" she asked.

"It's my turn, I guess," I answered shamefully.

"Your turn?"

"Yeah, each kid gets picked on by him."

"Has anyone else fought back?" my mother asked.

"None that I've seen!"

My mother smiled warmly.

"I didn't raise cowards, Ellard," she reminded me. "After today, this will no longer be a conversation, you understand me?"

"Yes, but what am I supposed to do? I'm really scared!"

"Baby," she said lovingly, putting her hands on my shoulders. "The next time this boy kicks or hits you, I want you to punch him until you can't punch anymore!"

"Punch him?" I asked, thinking of how I'd never fought anyone.

"Yes, the only way to deal with a bully is to fight back to show him you're not scared. Now, go upstairs and get ready for dinner..."

I had doubts about my mother's advice, but I made up my mind to face Rowan.

The following morning, I arrived at school to play with my friends. Like clockwork, Rowan rode in on his skateboard.

"Hey, Ellard," he yelled and skated toward me. "You know what to do. Bend over!"

"Leave me alone," I responded.

Rowan hopped off his skateboard and strutted toward me.

"I will, right after this!" Rowan kicked me and laughed.

I balled up my fists, thinking about what my mother had said. "Keep punching until you can't punch anymore!"

As Rowan stood laughing with his goons, anger overcame me. I had enough. Without warning, I jabbed him in the chest. The crowd grew silent. Rowan's eyes grew wide with surprise. I then sent a storm of left jabs and right hooks to his face, and unable to stop, I pushed him over his skateboard, causing him to fall. I fell upon him and continued the beating. Everyone continued to watch and chanted, "Ellard...Ellard!" My teacher finally dragged me away from my bloody foe. She helped Rowan to his feet and escorted us to the principal's office.

A three-day suspension and no more fear of Rowan were the results of that day. From that day on, no one else feared the school bully.

Like Rowan, fear is not as tough as we believe. He cannot continue to keep kicking you if you decide to fight back. The following chapters reveal in detail the seven principles to help you build the courage you need to face your fears and improve the quality of your life.

Chapter 2
Choose

"Decision is a risk rooted in the courage of being free!"

-Paul Tillich

The foundation upon which our ability to move forward courageously sits is ***the power to choose***. The choices we make can bring us closer to or take us further from our happiness. Before I could move forward and begin healing from my divorce, overcome homelessness, and rebound from my financial loss and business failures, I had to ***first choose*** to do so.

The Power to Choose

"The greatest power that a person possesses is the power to choose."

-J. Martin Kohe

Despite the adversity we face, we can choose our next move. We can either choose to stand still (and let life continue without us) or move forward and reshape our lives. The power to choose is truly ours.

Fortunately, the power to shape our destinies ultimately rests in our own hands. While some may be tempted to relinquish this responsibility to others, hoping to evade accountability for the outcomes, such a mindset only serves to stifle our potential for growth and fulfillment. This misguided belief has hindered countless individuals from thriving and embracing the fullness of life. It's imperative that we never allow anyone else to dictate the path to restoring happiness in our lives.

~ Molested repeatedly and abused at the age of 11 by our stepfather and then pushed into the unwelcoming arms of foster care, my sister Shameka lived a life of confusion, shame, and hurt. Once girls her age discovered this secret, they mocked her and made her feel inadequate, dirty, and worthless. Many of them had gone as far as to claim that she would become a high school dropout and a prostitute.

Feeling alone, lost, and confused, Shameka had to make a tough decision: either meet the expectations set on her or choose a path that could change the trajectory of her entire life. Rather than drop out of school and accept the life of a streetwalker, Shameka earned her high school diploma and completed many other professional certifications. Encouragingly, she is now a well-respected executive in the healthcare field, married to the love of her life, and is a loving, protective mother of two beautiful daughters. "Giving up is what they expected me to do," Shameka said. "I chose to live a life of success and happiness at my own discretion and refused to be controlled by my past!"

There's liberation when you exercise your right to choose. Many of us unknowingly are bound spiritually, mentally, and emotionally because we have not decided about something or someone. Fear of the unknown is the most likely reason behind this indecision. Before we can restore happiness in our lives, we must make tough decisions. In the next parts, you'll find some decisions you might need to make to start moving forward.

Choose to accept it!

"I slept in denial and dreamt that the pain I endured was that of someone else! It wasn't...it was my own...a reality I had to accept!"

-Coach Ell

When disaster strikes, it's natural to want to deny or ignore the painful reality of the situation. We might convince ourselves that if we pretend it isn't happening, we can avoid feeling the full weight of its impact. But let's be honest - who are we really fooling? Who are we trying to protect when we bury our emotions? Denial only holds us back from confronting our troubles and moving forward.

~ Accepting my divorce didn't come easy. When my wife and I separated, I spent many weeks in loneliness, depression, and confusion. I had little contact with friends and family as I entered a routine of going to work and coming home to sit in a dark, quiet bedroom. I often whispered, "This is not happening...We could work this out!" In my heart, I refused to believe that my marriage had come to an end. From my perspective, there were no irreconcilable differences—just differences common between men and women. Even though my wife had told me repeatedly that she wasn't ever coming back home, I wouldn't accept her statement as the truth.

Committed to fixing the marriage, I invited her to dinners, requested in-person meetings, and often visited her mother's house with the hope of rekindling our love. Disappointment followed each heart-crushing reiteration of her prior remarks. Although emotionally crushed, I kept trying.

13

Following a year of no contact with each other, I finally had to accept and prepare for the inevitable: divorce. With sadness in my heart, I mailed her the divorce papers and a little note, which read:

"Ruxpin, it is not my desire to be divorced, but I'll set you free if you so desire. I can no longer keep us both from experiencing happiness. I apologize for not accepting this reality a year ago. I love you, take care, and goodbye!"

Choosing to embrace hurtful circumstances as they truly are, rather than clinging to how we wish them to be, demonstrates the power of acceptance. Acceptance serves as a crucial step forward from painful situations, initiating the healing process. Through acceptance, we pave the way toward reclaiming our happiness and experiencing newfound freedom. This freedom isn't merely liberation from denial; it's the freedom to reconstruct and revitalize the life that adversity has temporarily obscured.

Choose to forgive

"To forgive is to set a prisoner free and discover that the prisoner was you!"

-Lewis B. Smedes

Forgiving those who have caused us pain can be incredibly challenging. It often feels easier and more satisfying to distance ourselves from those individuals rather than extend forgiveness.

~ A blood-curdling scream from my sister awakens me. My heart pounds loudly. Fear grips me. "Here we go again," I whisper nervously, jumping out of my bed and running to my sister's bedroom, ready to face my greatest enemy. I burst through the door.

"Get the hell off of her!" I holler, pushing my stepfather's naked, black, and sweaty body off my helpless, 11-year-old sister.

"You lil' muthafucka!" he slurs, struggling drunkenly to his feet, throwing on his trousers.

My sister cries as she lays helplessly in the fetal position. My mother sleeps peacefully while I'm left dealing with her worthless excuse for a man.

"Bring your ass back here!" my stepfather yells, chasing me into my room.

Trapped and with no way of escape, I find myself cowering in the corner, my gaze fixed on him as he leans against the doorway, his stance unsteady. His pants hang loosely on his hips, his eyes ablaze with a menacing red glow as he takes aim at me, unleashing his fury as though he were a .45 caliber bullet. Trembling uncontrollably, I raise my eyes to meet those of the towering, enraged figure before me, his fist poised like a sledgehammer ready to strike. I draw in a deep breath, attempting to steady my nerves.

"You're going to learn not to fuck with me!" he yells.

I shut my eyes tight, drowning in the echoes of my siblings' cries reverberating throughout the room. Despite the dread churning within me, I summon the strength to lift my chin, bracing myself for the impending onslaught of unjust punishment. Clenching my teeth with determination, I raise my head defiantly, almost daring this brutality to be the end of me.

In the blink of an eye, his fist crashes into my underdeveloped jaw, sending a jolt of searing pain coursing through me. My tongue collides harshly with my teeth as the force knocks me off balance, and I crash to the unforgiving floor, my face bearing the brunt of the impact. Before I can recover, two powerful kicks pummel into my stomach, driving the air from my lungs and painting the ground crimson with the blood that spills from trembling lips.

"Get up, you lil' faggot!" he says, picking me up by my blood-soaked t-shirt.

"I didn't do nothing!" I cry out, tears streaming from my swollen eyes.

"You're such a little bitch!" he laughs. "You could never be my son!"

His hand wraps around my throat like a vice, a sinister smile displaying on his lips as he tightens his grip. Darkness begins to creep in around the edges of my vision, threatening to consume me entirely. I muster every ounce of remaining strength, attempting to kick free from his grasp, but it's a futile effort. His strength dwarfs mine, leaving me feeling small and helpless in his overpowering presence.

With a cruel laugh, he mocks my pointless efforts to break free and forcefully hurls me across the room. I hit the ground hard, trembling from the impact, as blood begins to pool around me. My head throbs with intense pain, each heartbeat amplifying the agony.

How can God exist? I ask myself as blood pours from my mouth.

As I lay motionless, crying heavily, my stepfather lifts me in the air once again. Pinning me against the wall, he brings his chiseled, cold face within inches of mine.

"So you are the protector of the family, huh?" he laughs. "You see nigga, I run this damn house. Like I told you before, you ain't shit, and you'll never be shit! Each time you fuck with me, I'm gonna fuck you up!"

"So, is this what a man does?" I ask hoarsely. "I hope you die!"

"Nigga—what?" he yells.

My stepfather tosses me into a wall across the room and rushes over to prevent me from standing. Hunching over me, he cocks back his fists, preparing to punch me again.

"Had enough, you bastard?" he asks.

I hold my peace as tears sooth my busted, dry lips.

"Not so tough now, are you, Ellard?"

He waits for a few moments, turns off the light, and exits my room.

"Now go to sleep," he yells from the hallway.

My six-year-old brother rushes to my aid.

"We don't deserve this hell," I whisper as my head rests against his. "I wouldn't wish this on any child."

"I know, big bro. It'll get better," he comforts.

"It hasn't gotten better yet, Vamp!" I struggle to speak. "It keeps getting worse!"

17

My brother's tears fall onto my swollen left eye. I close my eyes, trying to figure out what I possibly could have done to receive this kind of abuse. What did my sister ever do to be sexually abused by a grown man? "Take my life now, Lord," I whisper, unable to move. "I want to die!" Suddenly, my pain subsides. A sense of peace veils me. *Is this heaven*? *God, are you there*? Finally, no more anguish and pain. A terrifying shriek from my mother brings me back to a harsh reality: I'm not dead. I'm still in this miserable existence. Weak, I gently push away my brother and stand to my feet, holding my aching left side.

"What did I do?" my mother hollers.

Two sonic-boom slaps follow her question.

"Stay here," I say to my brother. "Don't move."

"Okay," he says.

I head to the hallway, bouncing back and forth between walls to keep from falling.

"Mom," I cry, swaying toward their bedroom.

As I step into the room, a scene of horror unfolds before me. My mother, her nightgown torn and blood dripping from her nose and lips, huddles in the corner. Without a moment's hesitation, I leap onto my stepfather's back, determined to shield her from further harm.

With seemingly no effort at all, he flings me onto my mother, our heads colliding with a sickening thud. Despite the pain, we cling to each other for comfort as the enraged figure advances toward us. The piercing cries of my three-year-old brother and sister echo through the room, drowning out the hateful words spewing from my stepfather's mouth yet failing to quell the fury burning within him.

"Leave us alone!" my mother cries hysterically as my stepfather reaches for me.

In a desperate bid to defend myself, I lash out and kick his hand away, but my actions only seem to enrage him further. With a vicious growl, he grabs hold of me and forces me to the ground, his grip like a vise. In a swift, brutal motion, he seizes a two-by-four from the nearby bed and brings it crashing down onto my back with bone-shattering force. The agony is excruciating, and I can't help but cry out in pain. But instead of showing remorse, he merely laughs cruelly before turning his attention to my mother, dragging her across the floor by her ankles with a chilling disregard for her well-being.

"Get up, bitch," he growls.

"Cheetah, why are you doing this?" she screams.

Amidst the chaos of my stepfather's tirade, two sharp knocks echo through the house, momentarily halting his attack. Through the curtains, flashing red and blue lights illuminate the room, signaling the arrival of an unexpected visitor. My stepfather's expression contorts into a grimace, his grip tightening as he presses his foot against the back of my neck, a silent warning to stay quiet and comply.

"You betta tell them nothin's wrong, or I will kill your son, you understand me?" he says quietly as he cuffs my mother's arm.

"Okay, Cheetah, whatever you say!" my mother says, frantically wiping away the blood and tears with a towel. "Just don't hurt my baby..."

I roll my swollen eyes upward. My little brother, Chris, cries as he trembles in the doorway, reaching out for me. I can only close my eyes and regret the fact that I am not strong enough to protect him, my mother, or my sister.

For more than 15 years, my animosity toward Cheetah consumed me utterly. He robbed my 11-year-old sister of her innocence, got us placed in foster care, and instilled in me a deep self-loathing for my failure to protect my family. I would have willingly sacrificed my life if it meant putting an end to the suffering we endured. As time passed, I became lost in a maze of tumultuous emotions, suffused with anger and insecurity, inadvertently repelling love and shutting out any notions of happiness.

After undergoing several years of spiritual counseling, which assisted me in navigating through the aftermath of my divorce and various personal hurdles, I found myself confronted with the chance to face my stepfather once more. This time around, I stood as a combat-trained Marine, far removed from the feeble 13-year-old child I once was.

On my way home, I received a call from my mother.

"Ellard," she said.

"Yes, mom," I answered.

"You won't believe what just happened."

"What," I responded.

"Cheetah called me," she said.

Anger overcame me.

"What! What in the hell did he want," I scolded.

"Just to talk, I guess, but I quickly hung up the phone."

I pulled over to the shoulder of the road, wondering how Cheetah got my mother's number.

"Give me his number," I ordered, grabbing a pen and a piece of paper from my armrest console.

"Okay, Ellard. It's..."

After getting off the phone with my mother, I stared at Cheetah's phone number, unsure of what to do. Filled with mixed emotions, I called Pastor Hay.

"Hey, Pastor," I uttered, "where are you?"

"I'm at the church, Preach," he responded.

"Can I meet with you?"

"Absolutely. What time are you thinking?" he asked.

"I'm on my way," I responded.

For years, I wondered what I would do if I were to see Cheetah again. *Kill him? Wound him? Let him live?* I had no idea.

When I arrived at the church, Pastor Hay met me at the door and ushered me inside.

"What's on your mind?" He asked in a fatherly tone, sitting next to me.

I talked to the pastor about my phone call with my mom and told him how upset I was feeling. He nodded and then stopped to think for a moment.

"Ellard," he said softly, "you have every right to feel the way you do. But I want to tell you something that you might not want to hear."

"Yeah, but go on," I responded.

"You haven't seen this man in years, and God has finally gotten you to a place where you're at peace. You're flourishing, and you are building a great life."

"And?" I said, waiting for the gut punch.

"You may come to find that life has given him the justice that you can't give him..."

Pastor Hay tried to calm me and encouraged me to see things differently. Even though he was right, I still felt a strong urge for revenge.

"I hear you, pastor. As always, thank you for the talk."

We shook hands and agreed to see each other on Sunday.

Reflecting on my talk with Pastor Hay, I pondered what he said. Did life really give Cheetah the swift justice he was due? With each passing thought, my curiosity grew stronger.

Inhaling deeply, I summoned the courage to dial the number of my longstanding foe.

"Hello," a familiar voice answered. "Who's this?"

"Ellard," I said assertively.

"Ellard?" his voice cracked. "Hey, son, how are you? It's been a long time..."

Cheetah wanted to talk more, but I interrupted him, especially when he asked about my sister, Shameka.

"Look," I said, "I didn't call to chit-chat, but I think it's important that we meet in person."

"That would be great," he said excitedly. "What do you have in mind?"

"The sooner, the better," I replied, as I had a trip to Saint Marten planned in less than two weeks.

"Let's meet up Thursday."

"See you then," I confirmed.

The night before I had planned to meet up with Cheetah, I tossed and turned, wondering what justice, if any, life had given him. I couldn't wait to find out.

I picked up Cheetah early Thursday morning from a homeless shelter located in Downtown Seattle. It was the first sign of justice served, I thought. As he got into the car, I grasped the small screwdriver hidden in my jacket pocket, ready to end him if provoked. We greeted each other and remained silent until we arrived at a local restaurant.

After the hostess sat us, I wasted no time to break the awkward silence between Cheetah and me.

"Look here," I said sternly, staring into his aged eyes, leaning forward. "I don't like you and don't want to talk to you more than

I have to. I have several questions to ask, and how you answer them will determine the outcome of this meeting."

Cheetah nodded his head slowly, leaned back, and folded his hands on the table.

"Son," he said calmly, "ask me anything you want."

I had a laundry list of questions to ask Cheetah, such as, *Why did he abuse my mother? Why did he molest my sister? Why did he introduce us to such a horrible life?*

Every answer infuriated me, forcing me to relive each horrific moment. I felt some answers were excuses, and others were meaningless. Blaming his behavior on drugs, alcohol, and his abusive childhood wasn't good enough for me. But I continued the conversation.

As he explained his past actions and unacceptable behavior, Cheetah said something that stunned me, placing me in an unusual calm state.

"Ellard," he continued, "there's nothing I can say that will change the pain I caused you and the family. Reflecting on the life I led and the people I hurt, I sought God and got saved in 1995."

My hate shattered; my heart filled with pity. Sitting across from me was the man I wanted to rid the world of. As I dried my eyes, I continued to listen, realizing how correct Pastor Hay was. Life had given Cheetah the type of justice that I couldn't. He lived in a homeless shelter, he had become disabled, and he had to register as a sex offender everywhere he resided. Regaining my composure, I stared into Cheetah's sorrow-filled eyes and said, "I forgive you, and I hope God has mercy on you." We finished our drinks and parted ways, never to cross each other's paths again.

Forgiving my stepfather was emotionally draining, yet essential for my healing journey and the pursuit of the happiness I craved and rightfully deserved.

Many find it hard to forgive those who hurt them because forgiveness isn't easy—it's a spiritual process. When someone wrongs us, our first instinct is often to seek revenge, but this only keeps us trapped, blocking love and happiness. Have you forgiven those who hurt you? Have you forgiven yourself? Remember, true happiness comes when you learn to forgive.

Choose to love

"On the meadows of sorrow lays my heart, waiting to be connected to its rightful owner!"

-Donell Thomas

We've all experienced heartbreaking stories of investing our time, money, and emotions into relationships, only to find ourselves shattered in the end, haven't we? These experiences can bring about significant changes. Our eating habits might shift—we might lose our appetite entirely or find solace in overindulging. We become disoriented and uncertain about our next steps. Doubts plague us as we question what led to the abandonment, causing us to feel a profound loss of self-worth.

~ After my divorce, I swore off getting close to anyone again. Yet, much to my surprise, I found myself breaking that promise.

Milana and I had known each other since we were teenagers, but our lives took different paths until my marriage fell apart. It was then that she re-entered my life as more than just a friend; she became my confidant, my anchor. Her gentle demeanor, compassionate heart, and many other wonderful qualities, along with the presence of her darling daughters, helped me navigate through the pain of my divorce and find healing.

Regrettably, a relationship that held so much potential never blossomed into the beautiful partnership we envisioned. External forces, our failure to seek guidance from a higher power, stubbornness, profound differences in perspectives, and ineffective communication all played a role in dismantling the fragile foundation upon which our hopes rested. Despite our intimate compatibility and spiritual connection, we faltered in overcoming the obstacles that loomed before us.

Despite grappling with familiar emotions of rejection, sadness, anger, and betrayal, I recognized the importance of maintaining a hopeful outlook. While shielding my heart seemed like a protective measure, I understood that closing myself off entirely would only deprive me of the love I rightfully deserved. With each heartbreak, I embraced the opportunity to grow as a student of love. I emerged from these painful experiences with greater wisdom, compassion, and sensitivity toward a woman's needs, nurturing a deeper desire to be understanding and empathetic.

Thankfully, after finding healing, I summoned the courage to open my heart again, leading me to discover a remarkable woman affectionately named Mrs. Kimberly Thomas.

Love is a complex phenomenon, both deeply satisfying and perplexing. Its influence surpasses our understanding, encompassing more than mere verbal declarations or physical intimacy. Love is characterized by selflessness, forgiveness, kindness, humility, and enduring patience. It involves accepting our partner's imperfections, understanding their significance in our lives, and consistently making them feel cherished, valued and accepted. Unfortunately, many of us miss out on experiencing this beautiful gift due to various obstacles.

Firstly, our love tends to be conditional, meaning we remain with our partners primarily for our own gain, whether it's financial stability, social status, or any other factor that neglects the true essence of an individual's heart, mind, and soul. The moment our self-serving motives are jeopardized, we're quick to abandon the relationship. In the meantime, we devalue our partners for their failure to sustain the energy or titillation that initially drew us to them.

Secondly, it's common for the individuals we desire to differ from those to whom we are naturally drawn. For instance, as a man, my ideal partner may encompass qualities such as financial savvy, intellectual stimulation, beauty, devotion to God, a passion for travel, and a sense of purpose. However, I might find myself drawn to someone whose appeal lies solely in their physical appearance despite exhibiting traits like frequent profanity, ongoing intimate connections with previous partners, and other qualities indicating potential incompatibility. Similarly, a woman might yearn for a sensitive, ambitious, loving, and trustworthy partner with a strong spiritual foundation, only to be attracted to men who exhibit traits such as dishonesty, verbal and physical abuse, infidelity, and lack of ambition.

So why do we find ourselves entangled with these individuals? There are several reasons: a) we may perceive their potential to evolve into the ideal partners we desire; b) we might believe we don't deserve the partners we truly want; or c) we could be convinced that having our desired partners in our lives is simply unattainable. Consequently, we invest years of love and effort into relationships with partners who may never reciprocate our feelings in the same way.

Thirdly, many of us have endured heartache in the past, having loved deeply only to face abuse, betrayal, neglect, and infidelity from those we trusted with our hearts. We've been taken advantage of, felt unappreciated, and left to pick up the shattered pieces of our lives. Consequently, we shy away from the idea of opening our hearts again. The pain and exhaustion of past relationships cast a shadow over our belief in the possibility of finding true love. Yet, if we find ourselves feeling this way, we must examine the patterns in the people we've chosen to let into our lives. The root of the problem often lies within ourselves, not in the individuals we've loved.

However, it's crucial not to close ourselves off emotionally from a world brimming with potential partners who could fulfill our deepest desires for love and companionship. Despite the scars left by past relationships, we deserve to welcome love into our lives without allowing fear to hold us back. Instead, let's view each painful experience as emotional sandpaper, refining our understanding and expectations of love and ultimately guiding us toward deeper and more fulfilling relationships.

Choose to dream again

"Life is full of beauty. Notice it. Notice the bumble bee, the small child, and the smiling faces. Smell the rain, and feel the wind. Live your life to the fullest potential, and fight for your dreams."

-Ashley Smith

Life's challenges often compel us to shelve our dreams, relegating them to the realm of "What if?" while we lean on excuses and alibis. However, regardless of the obstacles you face, it's important to recognize that you still have the power to pursue and fulfill your dreams.

~ As a child, I dreamt about becoming an influential speaker, writer, and businessman. I would remove myself mentally from my abusive and impoverished surroundings, go to my room, and fantasize about encouraging kids and other people to overcome their own tragedies. Although I did not know how I would achieve my aspirations, I never forgot about my dream; I am now living it.

Why do we abandon our dreams? Perhaps because they seem too distant or require resources and support to which we don't have access. Perhaps we allow obstacles to divert our attention, and we become overly concerned with the opinions of others rather than staying focused on our aspirations.

Instead of allowing our dreams to wither away or remain unfulfilled, imagine daring to breathe life into them. What if we defied the constraints of our current circumstances and took a leap of faith to pursue what truly ignites our passion? There's a chance we could achieve remarkable success. However, the sad truth is that many of us never realize our dreams, all because of that notorious villain, Ol' Man Because.

Ol' Man Because is the ultimate dream killer. Whenever we muster the courage to chase after our desires, he inundates us with a barrage of ludicrous excuses. These excuses act as poison, suffocating our dreams until they lie dormant, never to awaken again. Here are some of the common excuses Ol' Man Because employs to strangle our ambitions:

Because I'm too old...

Because I don't have enough money...

Because I don't have the time...

Because I can't do it...

Because the timing is wrong...

Because I will next time...

Because it takes money to make money...

Because I have a handicap...

Because I'm divorced...

Because I'm too depressed...

Because I don't speak well...

Because I've been bankrupt...

Because I have horrible credit...

Because no one wants me...

Because I'm out of a job...

Because I'm scared...

Because something may happen...

Because I've been incarcerated...

Because I don't have a degree...

Because they don't want me to succeed...

Because I made some bad decisions...

Because of the economy...

Regardless of your present situation, you possess the power to turn any dream into a tangible reality. Hardships and obstacles will impede your progress only if you permit them to. Consider this: the magnificent cities and serene shorelines we admire across the world were once someone else's dreams. Shouldn't you start living out yours?

Choose to take action

"Take action when opportunity offers its hand."

-Thomas Donald

Achieving happiness and living a fulfilling life requires proactive steps, not procrastination. Too often, we postpone progress in various aspects of our lives simply because we hesitate to act.

"I will wait until..."

"Some day, I will begin..."

"One of these days..."

Waiting for the *perfect* moment to take action toward restoring happiness or achieving success in your life may never happen. The truth is, the best time to pursue the life you want is right now, not some indefinite point in the future. Therefore, you're faced with a decision: will you be like Myron, the diligent ant who takes proactive steps, or like Willy, the grasshopper who procrastinates and lets opportunities pass by?

~ In the lively seasons of spring and summer, Myron, the diligent ant, eagerly ventures out into the bustling world, teeming with towering obstacles and formidable challenges. His unwavering determination propels him forward as he tirelessly strives to secure his well-being and fulfill his objectives, knowing that failure is never an option.

Amidst the scorching heat of the pavement and the relentless passage of time, Myron persists as he strides across the perilous plains. Despite encountering barren landscapes, he refuses to yield; instead, his determination intensifies, his focus sharpening with each step. Despite his legs aching and his feet blistered and sore, Myron presses on, driven by an unwavering resolve. Just when he feels nearly defeated, a glimmer of hope emerges—a bounty of food awaits him atop a distant hill.

"Wow!" he exclaims, his breath coming in ragged gasps, a mix of exhaustion and excitement coursing through him. "Only a few more feet to go," he whispers to himself, bolstered by newfound confidence that surpasses his fatigue. With sweat pouring down his brow, he summons every ounce of strength to ascend the hill, his determination unwavering. Finally, he reaches the summit and throws his arms skyward in triumph.

"The struggle was worth it," he declares, tears of victory mingling with the sweat on his face as he revels in the hard-earned fruits of his labor.

Unlike his diligent friend Myron, Willy spends his days basking in the warmth of the spring and summer sun, squandering his time in idle pursuits. He sees no harm in procrastinating, always believing there will be another day to get things done. Instead of taking proactive steps, Willy relies on borrowing from others and postponing his responsibilities for another time. "I know I should be working, but I can do it tomorrow," he reassures himself. "I have plenty of friends who will help me out if I need anything!"

Lost in his carefree existence, Willy fails to notice the passage of time slipping through his fingers. Days turn into weeks, weeks into months, until suddenly, the vibrant colors of autumn fade into the bleakness of winter. Reality hits hard as Willy finds himself facing the harshness of the colder seasons, regretting his decision to delay action. Struggling with hunger and shelter, he scurries through wet and frosty terrains, desperately hoping for the opportunities of the sunny months to resurface—but they never do.

Exhausted and weakened by his own neglect, Willy seeks refuge at Myron's doorstep, begging for shelter and assistance. However, Myron, recognizing the consequences of Willy's choices, sadly shakes his head and closes the door. Left to fend for himself in the unforgiving elements, Willy succumbs to freezing temperatures and starvation, his days of leisure leading to nothing but despair and regret.

This story serves as a poignant reminder of the stark contrast between those who seize opportunities with action and those who languish in the inertia of indecision. Like Myron, many of us will bravely confront our setbacks, dust ourselves off, and embark on the journey of rebuilding our businesses and reinvesting in our dreams, undeterred by past financial failures. With unwavering determination, we declare, "Enough is enough," and actively seek ways to reclaim the happiness and fulfillment we rightfully deserve.

In contrast, individuals like Willy will sadly find themselves consumed by regret, anguish, and unhappiness as they squander precious time with procrastination. Caught in the cycle of "Maybe tomorrow," they watch as each day slips away, never seizing the opportunities that lie before them.

Taking action isn't just a one-time decision; **it's a way of life**. While some of us will adopt the mindset of resilience and resourcefulness, continuously striving to rebuild and pursue our aspirations, others will remain stagnant, finding comfort in inaction. Regardless of our choice, we must recognize that our outcomes are a direct reflection of our actions—or lack thereof.

Choose to have faith

"Faith is a knowledge within the heart, beyond the reach of proof."

-Kahlil Gibran

Have you ever found yourself at a loss for what to do when it feels like everything is crumbling around you? Have you noticed that despite your best efforts to improve a situation, it only seems to deteriorate further? The secret to weathering life's storms lies in having faith.

For some, the concept of "faith" may be synonymous with belief in a higher power or God. While this is indeed part of it, faith extends beyond that narrow definition. It encompasses a steadfast belief—free from doubt—in both the indomitable spirit within us and the presence of a higher spiritual power guiding us from above.

~ I often found myself contemplating quitting the commercial real estate industry. The behavior of Coach, coupled with his lack of clear direction, left me feeling frustrated and disheartened. Fed up and on the brink of confronting my so-called mentor, I sought guidance from my pastor, Gary Hay, Sr.

"Please pick up the phone," I whisper, hands shaking.

"Hello," Pastor Hay answers.

"Hey, Pastor, it's Ellard."

"How's it going," he responds.

"I'm done with being here!"

There was no response.

"Hello," I say, making sure the call hadn't dropped.

"I'm here," Pastor says.

"Well?" I say, growing agitated.

"Ellard, I don't think God brought you all the way up there for this not to work out in your best interest."

"Well, before you jump ahead of yourself, let me tell you what's going on..."

I open the floodgates on my pastor. I let him know how rude and ornery Coach has become. I really want him to give me the "OK" to leave. He doesn't. Instead, he asks two questions:

"Preach," he says, "Have you achieved the goal you set out for?

"Umm, no!" I answer, rolling my eyes.

"Are you willing to live with the idea of quitting before you achieve it?"

"No," I grunt.

"Well, despite all the things that are going on, remember you are a child of the Most High. Do you remember the attributes that God has given you as stated in 2nd Timothy?"

"Yes...'For he has given us a spirit of power, and of love, and a sound mind,'" I recite.

"So you know your power lies in faith. Faith will get you through when circumstances appear to prevail or dominate you."

"You're right," I mumble.

"Very well. Remember, *faith without works is dead*!"

"Thank you, Pastor."

"Alright!"

After ending the call, I slipped my cell phone into the pocket of my shirt and began pacing around the block, lost in thought. As I mulled over my conversation with Pastor Hay, I realized he was right. I couldn't simply walk away until I had achieved everything I had set out to accomplish. I needed to have faith in God and rely on His spirit within me to guide me toward success.

To live by faith means persistently pursuing your goals with the unwavering conviction that they will manifest in due time. Even in the face of setbacks or adversity, it's crucial to press forward, trusting in faith to guide you through the challenges that arise.

Alongside your other endeavors, it's vital to maintain faith as you pursue happiness. As Psalm 55:22 advises, we are encouraged to "cast our cares on the Lord," signifying that while we must take proactive steps to improve our circumstances, there comes a point where we must relinquish control and entrust the outcome to a higher power. This principle encourages us to strike a balance between diligent effort and surrender, recognizing that sometimes, despite our best efforts, we may be trying too hard to control the outcome.

How to live in faith

Living in faith presents its challenges, as it requires placing your focus on believing in an uncertain future.

Firstly, it's essential to firmly believe in your heart and mind that you deserve happiness, love, and success. Keep in mind that the happiness you're seeking may manifest in unexpected ways, not necessarily through the avenues you're currently pursuing. It may not be found within your present romantic relationship, job, or business endeavor. Therefore, it's crucial to keep your mind open to all possibilities and remain receptive to new paths that may lead you to fulfillment.

Secondly, after firmly establishing in your heart and mind that you deserve happiness, it's important to speak this belief into existence. With unwavering conviction, declare, "I will achieve my ultimate desire of _____!" However, be aware that your current circumstances may attempt to silence your affirmations and deter you from speaking your beliefs into reality.

Finally, it's crucial to maintain unshakable faith that your desires will ultimately come to fruition, even in the face of challenges and setbacks. Remember, the obstacles you encounter serve as steppingstones toward the life you envision. They have the potential to refine you, making you more resilient, stronger, and increasingly innovative. Keep this perspective in mind as you continue to pursue your happiness and strive for success.

We often encounter unforeseen challenges that disrupt our lives and bring about sorrow. However, despite these circumstances, we can rebuild our happiness through faith. It begins by embracing the belief that better days lie ahead, vocalizing this belief with conviction, and reaffirming it consistently. By integrating faith into your mindset and actions, you can lay the foundation for a brighter future and overcome the obstacles that stand in your way.

Choose to look forward

"Every man has a past. Whatever actions, words, deeds, challenges, and problems that lay dormant in the bed of

yesterday should remain there eternally and only be called to memory for a purpose."

- Coach Ell

Pain and suffering often deceive us, leading us to believe that there's something inherently wrong with us when, in reality, it's simply a natural part of being human. We're all susceptible to experiencing hurt inflicted by others, just as we, too, may unintentionally or intentionally cause pain to those around us. It's essential to recognize that experiencing hurt doesn't diminish our worth or value as individuals; rather, it's a shared aspect of the human experience.

I was taken aback when a dear friend shared something rather puzzling with me. She admitted that she found a strange comfort in replaying instances where she was mistreated because it reinforced her belief that she was unworthy of happiness. Allow me to share her story:

~ For months, my husband's affectionate touch had become a distant memory. His constant business travels kept him away, leaving me feeling lonely and unloved. While I respected his dedication as a provider and father, his lack of response upon returning home left me feeling neglected and insecure. Despite my doubts, I tried to dismiss any suspicions of infidelity and instead focused on rekindling our intimacy. I went to great lengths to entice him, wearing his favorite lingerie, enveloping myself in his preferred scent, and setting the scene with candles and roses, hoping to reignite the passion between us.

As I lovingly caressed his back and tenderly kissed his neck one evening, my husband abruptly rose from the bed. His gaze pierced through me, filled with a mix of anguish and disdain, as he uttered words that cut deeper than any knife. In that moment, the man I had loved and cherished, the father of our children, shattered my world with the most devastating confession.

Facing away from me, he remained silent as I implored him to share the source of his anguish. With a heavy heart and vacant expression, he finally turned to meet my gaze and uttered words that felt like a dagger to my soul.

"There's no easy way to say this," he began, his voice trembling with emotion. "But I've fallen in love with another woman, and she's carrying my child..."

Stunned into silence, I sat on the edge of the bed, unable to find the words to respond. Meanwhile, my husband, overcome with remorse, offered a feeble apology before quietly exiting the room. Fueled by a whirlwind of emotions, I bolted after him, my voice shaking with desperation as I pleaded for answers. "What did I do wrong? Whatever it is, I can fix it!" I cried out as he reached for the car keys, his gaze hardened with resolve.

With a heavy heart, he turned to face me one last time, leaving me standing there, trembling and bewildered. In the days that followed, my mind was consumed by a relentless barrage of unanswered questions. *What had I done to deserve this? Was I no longer enough for him? Was he no longer attracted to me?* The doubts and insecurities gnawed at my soul, casting a shadow of doubt over everything I thought I knew about our relationship.

As of the writing of this book, Julia finds herself five years into her divorce, yet the lingering question of what went wrong continues to haunt her. Consumed by the belief that her actions played a pivotal role in the demise of her marriage, she remains entrenched in sorrow, unable to shake off the weight of her loss. Despite the passage of time, Julia remains fixated on the past, unable to envision a future filled with the promise of new beginnings and potential love. Her heart remains closed off to the possibility of happiness with someone new as she grapples with the lingering shadows of her past.

Julia's anguish was unfounded; she bore no responsibility for the dissolution of her marriage. It was her husband who had faltered, succumbing to the allure of a younger companion and forsaking the integrity of their union. Blinded by his own insecurities, he failed to recognize Julia's inherent beauty and unwavering devotion. Instead of embracing her worth, Julia internalized her husband's shortcomings, shouldering the weight of his betrayal as her own.

Tragically, Julia remains oblivious to her own worth, unable to fathom the prospect of finding a partner who cherishes her affectionate and compassionate nature. Caught in the web of her past, she is unable to see the blessings that surround her in the present.

Reflecting on your past can be a double-edged sword. While memories offer comfort and nostalgia, they also have the power to entrap you in a cycle of longing and regret, halting your progress toward a brighter future. For some, dwelling on the past serves as a justification for destructive behaviors or unproductive habits, preventing them from moving forward and embracing the opportunities that lie ahead.

As life marches on, so must we. We cannot linger in the shadows of our past, endlessly chasing after partners who have chosen to depart or pining for jobs from which we've been let go. Likewise, we cannot wallow in self-pity over failed business endeavors nor allow the weight of past mistakes to shackle us with guilt and shame. Instead, we must summon the courage to forge ahead, leaving behind the burdens of yesterday and embracing the promise of tomorrow.

Moving forward requires a conscious decision to release the grip of the past and set our sights firmly on the path ahead. It means relinquishing the urge to dwell on what could have been and focusing instead on what can still be achieved. Only by looking forward with determination and resilience can we break free from the chains of regret and step into the boundless possibilities that await us.

The Choice is Yours

"Remember, there are no mistakes, only lessons. Love yourself, trust your choices, and everything is possible."

-Cherie Carter-Scott

Feeling nervous and uncertain about the future is a natural response to the unknown, but allowing these emotions to paralyze you can impede your progress. The key lies in making conscious choices that serve as the building blocks for rebuilding and reclaiming happiness in your life. Each decision, no matter how daunting, propels you forward on the path toward your aspirations.

Embracing the power of choice empowers you to take control of your destiny and steer your life in the direction of fulfillment and success. It's about making deliberate decisions that align with your values and aspirations, even in the face of uncertainty. By making the choice to prioritize your happiness and pursue your goals with determination, you set the stage for a brighter and more fulfilling future.

Chapter 3
Oppose Failure

"But there is suffering in life, and there are defeats. No one can avoid them. But it's better to lose some of the battles in the struggles for your dreams than to be defeated without ever knowing what you're fighting for."

-Paulo Coelho

In the preceding chapter, we explored the pivotal decisions required to initiate the process of rebuilding our lives. Yet, it's important to acknowledge that challenges and obstacles will inevitably arise along the way. When faced with adversity, the temptation to succumb to feelings of despair and resignation may be strong. However, yielding to such negative impulses is not the solution.

Instead, we must steadfastly oppose failure and refuse to surrender to defeat. It is through resilience and determination that we can rise above adversity and emerge victorious. By confronting challenges head-on and refusing to be deterred by setbacks, we pave the way for our triumph and ultimate success.

I had reached the age where I was no longer under the care of the foster care system, marking a significant transition in my life. Fortunately, during this uncertain period, I found refuge in the home of my best friend's mother—a true godsend who prevented me from facing the grim reality of life on the streets.

Despite my newfound stability, I harbored deep-seated resentment toward the child welfare system. After all, following my departure from the system, I was left to fend for myself without any assistance in securing housing or support. Therefore, when my youngest brother's caseworker requested a meeting with me, I was initially reluctant to comply.

However, upon learning that the purpose of the meeting was to discuss matters concerning my baby brother, I reluctantly agreed to meet with her. Despite my reservations, I recognized the importance of addressing the welfare of my sibling, setting aside my grievances for the sake of familial responsibility.

Stepping into Ms. Lane's office, I was immediately greeted by the musty odor that permeated the air. The room itself seemed frozen in time, with faded paint and graffiti adorning the walls and the table before me marred by countless scratches and scuff marks—a testament to the wear and tear of years of use. Despite the less-than-inviting environment, I settled into the chair opposite Ms. Lane, bracing myself for the conversation that lay ahead.

"Thank you for coming in," Ms. Lane said. "There's something important that we need to discuss."

"Okay," I responded anxiously.

"The State has decided to put the twins up for adoption!"

"What," I said, my heart racing. "What in the hell do you mean?"

"Once your mother terminated her parental rights, we attempted to place your siblings with members of your family. No one agreed to take them long-term. Adoption is the next logical move."

"Before you do this," I said, my eyes welling up with tears, "what can I do to stop this from happening?"

"Are you in a financial state to shelter and provide for them?"

"You know the answer," I said. "I make $5.75 an hour at a cookie shop. How in the hell am I supposed to take care of my siblings? Y'all didn't do anything for me when I aged out of foster care. I was homeless, and now you have the audacity to present me with this shitty offer. Got to hell, Ms. Lane."

Ms. Lane's eyes widened in surprise, a subtle indication that my reaction had caught her off guard. Despite her best efforts to maintain a professional demeanor, I could discern a flicker of uncertainty in her expression. It was as though my response had momentarily disrupted the façade of professionalism she sought to uphold. Despite her attempt to conceal her surprise, I could sense a subtle shift in her demeanor, hinting at her genuine reaction to my words.

"Unless you're in a financial position to provide for them," she re-engaged, "I strongly encourage you to join the military."

Join the military? The mere thought struck me as absurd. The idea of enlisting in the armed forces felt utterly outlandish, especially given my deep-seated skepticism and disdain for government institutions. My lack of respect extended beyond just state authorities; I harbored a profound distrust of federal governance as well. The notion of placing my faith in an entity that I viewed with such skepticism seemed downright ridiculous to me.

"Is this really my only option?" I murmured.

"Unfortunately, it is."

A wave of nausea washed over me, my stomach churning with a mix of disgust and sadness as I gazed at the woman before me. Her demeanor reeked of insensitivity, and I struggled to contain my rising frustration and anger. The mere sight of her filled me with an overwhelming sense of revulsion, making it difficult to maintain my composure in her presence.

"How about you give me a chance to get stable, and then we can have this conversation again?"

"I'll tell you this," she said. "How about I give you a year to get your affairs in order? Is this fair?"

"None of this is fair, but I guess I have to accept it..."

I exerted every ounce of effort to establish myself financially. Temporarily setting aside my college plans, I took as many shifts as I could. Climbing through the ranks, I attained the position of assistant manager, earning a modest wage of $6.25 per hour. Despite my relentless dedication, a year passed, and I found myself still far from achieving my financial objectives.

At my wit's end, I called Ms. Lane and said, "I will join the military if you promise to forfeit the adoption process."

"I'm glad to hear this," she said. "There's something I want you to know, though."

"What's that?" I responded.

"We were able to find your youngest sister a good home, but your brother, on the other hand, had to be placed in a group home."

Overwhelmed by the flood of this news, I reached my breaking point. The weight of the information bore down on me, rendering me speechless and unable to articulate the turmoil raging within me. My mind raced with thoughts of my brother, imagining the hardships he must be enduring. The mere thought of him left unprotected was enough to leave me vexed, consumed by a mixture of anguish, frustration, and helplessness.

As soon as I ended the call, waves of despair washed over me, and tears streamed down my face uncontrollably. The weight of the decision to leave my siblings behind weighed heavily on my heart, leaving me consumed by grief. However, amid the torrent of emotions, a steely resolve began to take shape within me.

Driven by a burning desire to provide a brighter future for my family, particularly my brother, I made a pivotal decision. With unwavering focus, I resolved to enlist in the Marine Corps, determined to embark on a path that would not only transform my own life but also pave the way for a better future for those I loved.

Joining the military marked the beginning of a challenging journey aimed at reuniting with my brother. Upon my return to Seattle following my military service, I wasted no time in meeting with my brother's caseworker. Armed with my bank statements and apartment lease, I hoped to demonstrate my readiness to provide him with a stable and loving home.

My optimism was quickly met with the harsh reality of the foster care process. Unfamiliar with its complexities, I was taken aback by the myriad of requirements and procedures I needed to navigate. It became apparent that securing my brother's placement with me would require more than just paperwork—it would demand a deep understanding of how to care for a child with special needs.

Driven to achieve my goal, I embarked on a journey of learning and preparation. I committed myself to attending the necessary classes and training sessions, recognizing that they were crucial steps on the path to bringing my brother home. Each class I attended served as a reminder of the challenges ahead but also as a testament to my unwavering dedication to providing my brother with a safe and nurturing environment.

I worked closely with my brother's caseworker, striving to meet every requirement and expectation placed before me. This included diligently completing the recommended foster care classes, where I absorbed valuable knowledge and skills essential for providing adequate care for my brother. Additionally, I willingly subjected my home to multiple inspections, ensuring that it met all the necessary safety and suitability standards.

Recognizing the importance of being fully prepared, I also sought out additional classes and training sessions as suggested by the caseworker. These supplementary sessions provided me with invaluable insights and practical strategies for effectively supporting and nurturing my brother, particularly given his special needs.

Throughout this process, my commitment to bringing my brother home remained unwavering. I understood that each step taken was not only a requirement but also a vital investment in his well-being and future happiness. By cooperating wholeheartedly and going above and beyond what was asked of me, I demonstrated my dedication to providing him with a loving and supportive home environment.

After enduring months of what felt like a never-ending game of "caseworker says," I reached a breaking point. Frustration and exhaustion consumed me, leaving me feeling defeated and emotionally drained. The entire foster care process seemed like an incomprehensible maze, with each new requirement and obstacle pushing me further to the edge.

As I navigated through the bureaucratic red tape, I couldn't shake the nagging sense of injustice. I couldn't understand why someone like me, who had never harmed a soul and only sought to provide a loving home for my brother, was subjected to such scrutiny and doubt. It was a stark contrast to the news stories I had seen, highlighting cases of criminal foster parents slipping through the cracks and causing harm to innocent children.

Despite my frustration and the sacrifices I had already made, including putting my college aspirations on hold, I remained steadfast in my determination to persevere. Countless hours were spent jumping through hoops and fulfilling every demand placed before me. Yet, as the pressure mounted and the obstacles seemed insurmountable, thoughts of quitting began to creep into my mind.

It was during one of these moments of self-doubt that my friend, Ce Ce, came to my rescue. Her support and encouragement reminded me of the reason behind my relentless pursuit: my unwavering love for my brother. Her words of wisdom and reassurance served as a beacon of hope in the darkness, reigniting the fire within me to press on despite the challenges.

"Ellard," she said as she wiped the tears from my eyes. "I know this is hard for you, and you've already sacrificed so much. I will continue to support you in whatever decision you make, but I know you've come too far to give up now!"

"You don't understand," I whimpered. "Why do I have to do all this crap? I don't know anyone else who had to go through these many ridiculous steps to become a foster parent!"

"That's true, but you have an opportunity to give your brother a better future. Besides, the Ellard I know will rise above this and make good on his promise to his mother. You said you wanted him before he turned 13, right?"

"Yeah," I said, taking a deep breath.

"Well, that's only a few months away. So, let's get this done and bring your brother home..."

As Ce Ce pressed a tender kiss to my forehead, her gaze loaded with affection, I felt a jolt of energy within me. Her genuine sincerity and boundless compassion seemed to awaken a dormant resolve deep within my soul. As she gracefully departed the room, leaving behind an aura of warmth, I found myself lifting my head high, infused with a newfound sense of vigor.

In that moment, I realized that I had made a solemn commitment to myself, one that I refused to let be derailed by the obstacles in my path. With a renewed perspective on the challenges before me, I tackled each hurdle with unbreakable determination. Despite the odds stacked against me, I persevered and completed all the necessary classes, getting custody of my brother as I had planned.

Failure often lurks in the shadows, ready to pounce at the slightest sign of progress in our journey toward our dreams and happiness. It seems to bask in our struggles and strives to obstruct our efforts. Its aim is not our success but our defeat. Yet, succumbing to the grip of hopelessness is akin to surrendering our dreams. By resigning ourselves to despair, we willingly relinquish our aspirations and consign ourselves to a fate dictated by fear and uncertainty.

Give Up on Giving Up

"No one attains perfection by merely giving up work."

-Bhagavad Gita

In the face of adversity, far too many of us succumb to the allure of failure all too swiftly. Instead of summoning the courage to stand firm and persevere in the pursuit of our goals, we often choose the path of least resistance, surrendering to the slightest hint of opposition. It's a common tendency to view our obstacles as insurmountable and our challenges as daunting threats to our progress.

What we often fail to recognize is the immense strength and resilience lying dormant within us. No matter how formidable the task may seem, you possess the inherent ability to overcome adversity and emerge victorious. It's not the magnitude of the challenge that determines your success but rather your unwavering determination and willingness to confront and surmount the obstacles in your path. With steadfast resolve and a courageous spirit, you can transcend any barrier and achieve the greatness that lies within your reach.

Amidst the festive cheer of the Christmas season, I was taken aback when my phone suddenly rang, the caller ID revealing a friend I hadn't connected with in what felt like ages. As I answered the call, the tone of his voice immediately caught my attention, striking me with surprise. This was not the composed and steady demeanor I had come to expect from him; rather, there was an unmistakable sense of urgency and distress underlying his words.

"Ellard," he says with sorrow.

"Yes," I answer, a little concerned.

"Things are not going as I had hoped," he says.

"Tell me what's going on…"

As I listened intently, I witnessed a stark contrast to the image of resilience and strength I had always associated with my friend. Over the phone, he unraveled before me, his voice trembling with emotion as he confided in me about the tumultuous challenges besieging both his personal and professional life. It was a revelation that shattered my perception of his staunch fortitude as he bared his soul, grappling with the overwhelming weight of his struggles.

His words painted a poignant picture of despair and disillusionment, as he expressed a profound desire to simply walk away from it all—to abandon not just his professional endeavors but also the people closest to him. In that vulnerable moment, it became abundantly clear that even the strongest among us are not immune to the crushing burden of life's trials and tribulations.

"JR," I respond. "I've known you for many years now, and I've never known you to quit anything. If it wasn't for you, I wouldn't have achieved many of my own goals."

"But this time," he sighs, "I've had enough!"

"Had enough—of what?"

"Her...the kids...the job...my life!"

A moment of silence breaks our intense dialogue.

"JR," I say calmly.

"What's up, Ell?" he says.

"If you're going to give up on something—give up on giving up!"

Again, silence takes over.

"Ellard, you're right! I never looked at it that way. Yeah, I should give up on giving up..."

It seemed that something I said resonated deeply with JR as his demeanor underwent a swift transformation. Within moments, a noticeable shift occurred in the tone of our conversation. He began to share his newfound perspective, emphasizing his decision to confront his challenges with resilience rather than allowing failure to dictate his path. It was evident that he had made a conscious choice to approach life with a renewed sense of determination and optimism.

Now, as I reflect on our conversation, I'm heartened to see JR embracing a brighter, more fulfilling life. By refusing to be defined by his setbacks, he has embarked on a journey toward greater happiness and contentment. His story serves as a powerful reminder of the transformative power of resilience and perseverance in the face of adversity.

80/20 Rule of Happiness and Success

"Make the best use of what is in your power, and take the rest as it happens."

-Epictetus

The Pareto Principle, often referred to as the 80/20 Rule or the "law of vital few," suggests that a significant portion of our outcomes can be traced back to a small fraction of our efforts or inputs. In essence, approximately 80 percent of the results we achieve are derived from just 20 percent of our actions or thoughts. This principle highlights the disproportionate impact that certain activities or thoughts—the so-called "vital few"— have on our overall well-being and success compared to the multitude of other factors at play.

Let's break down this concept further.

If I were to only focus on my problems for a part of my day (20 percent), I may encounter nothing but challenges (80 percent). Better yet, if I decided to do a few destructive activities because of my dissatisfaction with my life (20 percent), I may experience other unfavorable conditions stemming from my behavior (80 percent).

Essentially, your happiness and success hinge upon your thoughts and actions. The level of attention you devote to both, whether positive or negative, greatly influences the outcomes you experience. By being mindful of your thoughts and intentional in your actions, you enhance your ability to shape the trajectory of your life and attain the desired results. Conversely, neglecting to monitor and guide your thoughts and behaviors can lead to unintended consequences or undesirable outcomes. Thus, cultivating self-awareness and actively managing your mindset and actions are key components in achieving happiness and fulfillment.

Understanding Temporary Defeat

"Opportunity often comes in disguised in the form of misfortune, or temporary defeat."

-Napoleon Hill

When we invest our time and effort into pursuits like achieving financial stability or finding love, and we encounter outcomes that fall short of our expectations, it's easy to perceive these moments as failures. This perception doesn't always align with reality.

It's important to understand that setbacks and disappointments are not synonymous with failure. In fact, they often serve as crucial stepping stones on the path to success. They provide us with valuable insights, teach us important lessons, and ultimately contribute to our growth and resilience.

Success is not solely determined by the attainment of specific goals; it's also about how we respond to challenges and setbacks along the way. Embracing setbacks as opportunities for learning and growth, rather than viewing them as failures, allows us to maintain a positive outlook and continue progressing toward our aspirations. It's a reminder that setbacks are not roadblocks but rather detours that redirect us toward greater fulfillment and achievement.

Contrary to popular belief, failure is a state of mind born from the overwhelming pressure of adverse circumstances that lead us to quit. When we succumb to exhaustion and doubt, our efforts seem futile, and challenges appear insurmountable. Yet, what we often fail to understand is that our perception of failure is often self-imposed. Encouragingly, it's not failure that we often meet; it is *temporary defeat*.

Differentiating between temporary defeat and failure can be challenging because their outcomes may initially appear similar. However, they are fundamentally distinct. Failure occurs when you choose to give up entirely, relinquishing any hope of progress. On the other hand, temporary defeat encompasses obstacles that serve as opportunities for growth and self-discovery.

Temporary defeat presents us with challenges that are meant to test our resilience and resourcefulness. It prompts us to reassess our approach, seek support from others, and reconsider our perceptions of the situation. While temporary defeat may bear a resemblance to failure, it harbors hidden elements that are often overlooked: pivotal moments that prompt crucial changes in direction and setbacks that foster resilience and commitment.

Essentially, temporary defeat is not the end of the road but a detour on the path to success. It challenges us to adapt, learn, and grow stronger, ultimately propelling us forward toward our goals. Recognizing the distinction between temporary defeat and failure empowers us to persevere in the face of adversity and emerge stronger on the other side. Components of temporary defeat are turning points and setbacks.

Turning points

"The turning point in the process of growing up is when you discover the core of strength within you that survives all hurt."

-Max Lerner

An online medium defines turning points as "events marking a unique or important historical change of course or one on which important developments depends." Conversely, turning points are the emotionally and spiritually crippling events over which we have no control and cannot prevent from happening, such as the loss of loved ones and sudden illnesses.

~ Standing with his friends, a young boy watches a car with tinted windows drive slowly up the street. A masked individual pokes his head out of the window, aims a semi-automatic weapon at a nearby phone booth, and opens fire. Bystanders drop to the ground to avoid becoming victims. The 18-year-old man using the phone is not so lucky. Blood splatters on the phone booth windows as he lies and shakes on the cement floor. Witnessing this horrific scene, the young boy and his friends run to the teenager's aid. Crying aloud, the boy drops to his knees, cups the young man's head, and yells, "Someone help my brother!"

From the day of witnessing the slaying of his oldest brother, Matt became a neighborhood menace. Once a student who prided himself on academic achievement, Matt lost all hope of becoming an engineer. He often skipped school, engaged in petty fights, and sold drugs. Without his oldest brother's encouragement, he had become lost and confused. Life no longer held any appeal. The painful loss of his brother had blinded him from seeing a promising future. One of the school's counselors requested that I speak to him to see if I could help him. I obliged.

~ Sitting in a room, I wait for Matt. Loud, vulgar language from the hallway lets me know he has arrived. His counselor escorts him into the room and then leaves. Twisting his lips, Matt seats himself in a chair farthest away from me. I smile.

"Matt," I say. "I'm Ellard."

"So?" he says, folding his arms. "I've seen you around school. Why in the hell am I here? This is supposed to be detention."

"This is, but your counselor requested that we talk to each other."

"What the fuck for?" he yells.

"I think we have more in common than you think," I respond calmly.

Matt rolls his eyes upward, his anger strengthening its hold on him.

"I know how you feel," I respond, reflecting on the brutal death of my cousin.

"Know how I feel? You don't know anything about me! No one knows how the fuck I feel!"

"I know you're angry because you lost your brother a couple of years ago! Am I right?"

Matt's eyes fill with tears as he rises from his seat and stomps toward the door.

"I'm outta here!" he yells.

I close my eyes, bringing myself back to the day I lost my cousin.

"I was only a freshman when my cousin died," I begin telling my story. "Two weeks prior to his death, we had an altercation with some thugs over a misunderstanding. Trying to refrain from escalating the situation further, my cousin tried to excuse himself and mind his own business. One of the guys sucker-punched him in the face...This started a massive brawl..."

Matt returns to his seat and scowls but remains attentive. I continue.

"And two weeks later, as we discussed my plans following my graduation, we heard two gunshots. My cousin shoved me to the ground, falling on top of me moments later... He died in the ambulance..."

Matt and I continued to confide in each other about the pain we were feeling. Despite his reluctance to embrace the behavior typical of an out-of-control teenager, Matt found himself resorting to destructive and inappropriate actions as a means of coping. Recognizing the need for a positive change, I encouraged him to draw strength from the supportive words of his brother and to view his current struggles as a turning point on his journey toward achieving his lifelong aspirations.

Through numerous one-on-one meetings, I guided Matt toward reclaiming his focus on his dream of becoming an engineer. With determination and resilience, he committed himself to this goal. Impressively, by the time he reached his senior year, Matt not only earned an academic scholarship to his desired university but also emerged as a vocal advocate for ending youth violence

Matt's story exemplifies the transformative power of perseverance and self-belief. Despite encountering significant obstacles, he refused to give in to despair and instead chose to pursue positive change. Through his dedication, Matt not only achieved personal success but also became an inspiring figure for others facing similar challenges

The death of Matt's brother was a pivotal point in his life. Could he have controlled or prevented his brother's death? No, but Matt believed he had failed because he couldn't stop the tragic event from happening. How many times have you "felt" like a failure because you couldn't prevent something disastrous from happening to those you love?

We cannot predict the moment when we will lose the people in our lives to circumstances out of our control. Still, loss has an unpleasant way of making us feel like failures despite this truth. The more responsibility we take for the circumstances we cannot control, the deeper into depression we'll sink and the angrier we'll become. Eventually, we'll lose faith, hope, and the desire to live as we turn to destructive activities.

Despite the point where you are in your life right now, you can turn around your situation by moving forward while working through your pain. In the memory of those we lost, we owe it to them (and ourselves) to move on.

Setbacks

"People who make money often make mistakes, and even have major setbacks, but they believe they will eventually prosper, and they see every setback as a lesson to be applied in their move towards success."

-Jerry Gillies

Setbacks serve as pivotal moments that afford us the opportunity to reassess, reevaluate, and refine our strategies for rebuilding our lives. These setbacks encompass various challenges, including financial losses, unexpected familial shifts, and the failure of business endeavors. For instance, experiencing a series of unfavorable investments shouldn't deter us from exploring alternative financial avenues that align with our goals. Similarly, the arrival of new family members shouldn't hinder our pursuit of our dreams. Furthermore, being laid off from a job shouldn't keep us from exploring our talents and potential paths for earning the income we deserve.

~ Eager and full of ambition, Devin and a group of acquaintances embark on a venture to boost their wealth through investments in the commodities market. Initially, their efforts yield swift financial gains, fueling their confidence in the venture. However, blinded by their overconfidence, Devin and his friends decide to double down on their investments, pouring all their remaining resources into the endeavor. Unfortunately, this bold move proves to be a mistake, leading to a devastating financial collapse.

Dismissing their losses with a casual shrug, Devin's acquaintances retreat to the comfort of their affluent families, viewing their financial setbacks as inconsequential. However, Devin finds himself abandoned, grappling with his misfortune in solitude.

Alone in a dimly lit hotel room, Devin sits with his thoughts, his mind consumed by uncertainty. With only about fifty dollars left in his wallet, he gazes out of the window, tears welling in his eyes as the weight of his decisions bears down on him. "What have I done?" he whispers, gripped by fear and apprehension about the uncertain road ahead.

As Devin continues to gaze out of the window, memories of his rebellious youth flood his mind. He recalls how he had always refused to accept undesirable circumstances, consistently finding ways to overcome them. Determined not to wallow in self-pity, he straightens his posture, takes a deep breath, and reaches for a pen and a sheet of notebook paper.

Over the course of two hours, Devin meticulously compiles a list detailing his unique attributes, passions, and the names of acquaintances whom he hopes will rally behind his vision. With unwavering determination, he begins to outline a comprehensive business plan. Fueled by ambition and resilience, he dedicates himself to realizing his dreams.

After years of tireless effort, Devin transformed himself into a successful real estate investor, generating millions for himself and his clients. His story stands as a testament to the power of resilience, resourcefulness, and determination in the face of adversity.

Despite facing significant setbacks and the loss of his finances, Devin refused to succumb to defeat. While others may have been tempted to abandon their aspirations, Devin remained steadfast in his determination to achieve his vision of becoming a successful entrepreneur. Unlike his acquaintances who may have resigned themselves to failure, Devin chose to listen to the voice of his inner champion, echoing the resolute mantra: "I will not fail!"

Setbacks are not merely stumbling blocks but rather steppingstones on the path to success. They are not intended to lead to failure but rather to prompt us to refine our strategies based on past experiences. In the face of setbacks, we are compelled to delve deeper into our resources, widen our perspective, and intensify our focus.

While some may argue against this perspective, consider the following: How would you truly gauge the measure of your strength and resilience if you effortlessly achieved every goal and desire without encountering challenges? It is through overcoming adversity that you discover the extent of your capabilities and the depth of your determination. Without challenges, you would never fully realize your potential or appreciate the journey of growth and self-discovery that accompanies it.

~ Amid the turmoil of a failing housing market, builders like Danny Sorencho found themselves grappling with financial hardship. As financial institutions teetered on the brink of collapse, Danny, too faced the grim reality of having to foreclose on each of his housing projects. However, amidst this sea of adversity, there remained one beacon of hope—the abandoned five-bedroom home he and his father had designed and constructed years ago.

Standing before the weather-beaten structure, its worn facade in desperate need of repair, Danny reflects on the days when he worked alongside his father. He recalls his father's belief that anything could be built with determination and resourcefulness. "As long as you have your wits about ya, the two hands God gave ya, and a reason to do it, that's all you really need!" his father's words echo in his mind.

With a deep breath and a smile, Danny surveys the dilapidated 2,800-square-foot home. Regardless of its current state, he sees potential despite the decay. Drawing upon his remaining resources, he resolves to breathe new life into the aging structure. With each repair and renovation, he honors the legacy of his father's teachings and the enduring spirit of resilience.

As Danny puts the finishing touches on the transformed dwelling, a vision begins to take shape in his mind. Inspired by the rejuvenation of his own home, he imagines starting a remodeling and consulting firm. With the rebuilt home serving as his office, Danny embarks on a new chapter, driven by a passion to restore and revitalize not just buildings but also the dreams and aspirations of those he serves.

Setbacks have the remarkable ability to offer us a glimpse of how we can enhance and reclaim our lives, much like they did for Danny. They serve as reminders to revisit neglected areas of our lives that need attention, whether it be in matters of love, aspirations, or other facets of our existence. While it's natural to reflect on what went wrong during these challenging moments, it's equally important to extract valuable lessons from them.

These lessons serve as guiding beacons, shaping our approach to future endeavors. Instead of dwelling on defeat and asking disempowering questions like "Why me?" we should shift our focus to more empowering inquiries: "How can I turn this situation to my advantage?" "What steps can I take now to move closer to my goals?" "How can I rise above this setback?"

By posing such questions, we liberate our minds from a victimized state and pave the way for constructive action. Our minds become attuned to solutions and strategies for progress, empowering us to chart a course forward with confidence and resilience.

Committing to the End Result

"It is not in the stars to hold our destiny but in ourselves."

-William Shakespeare

Unfortunately, many of us view setbacks and turning points as valid reasons to throw in the towel. For those predisposed to seeking excuses, giving up becomes all too easy. Yet, if we entertain thoughts of quitting, a myriad of excuses will readily present themselves. Our ability to persevere through challenges and adversity hinges on our unwavering commitment to our desired outcomes. If we approach the pursuit of a happier, more fulfilling life with lukewarm enthusiasm, setbacks—no matter how minor or significant—will inevitably derail us.

However, when our focus is firmly fixed on achieving our goals, we tap into reservoirs of resilience that enable us to weather the storms of disappointment and hardship. Despite the pain and pressure urging us to quit, our determination remains steadfast. If love is our aim, we will unearth pathways to receive it. If financial security is our goal, we will delve deep within ourselves to dig up the talents and ideas necessary to attain it.

Ultimately, it is our immutable commitment to our desired outcomes that fuels our resilience and propels us forward, even in the face of adversity.

~ Waving to her friends in the crowd, Lisa takes her mark on the track, hoping to maintain her undefeated record in the 200-meter hurdles. Staring straight ahead and positioned to take off, Lisa waits for the sound of the cap gun. "Runners on your mark," the heavyset referee yells. "Get set...." He pulls the trigger.

Lisa dashes to the lead, jumping over the first set of hurdles and then the second. It appears she'll claim victory once again.

In mid-air, Lisa gets a cramp in her right leg and lands hard, dropping onto the dusty track. Her trainer darts out to her rescue. Intead of letting him assist her, Lisa pushes him away and stands on her feet. In agony, she finishes the race in last place.

Sitting on the bleachers, rocking back and forth in pain and knee bleeding, Lisa looks up at me as I approach her.

"Why didn't you step off the track?" I ask. "Clearly, everyone would've understood if you couldn't finish."

Lisa looks up at me with her sparkling, hazel eyes.

"Everyone but me," she says with a smile. "A true champion must complete the race despite opposition. Sure, I'm hurt, but finishing meant more to me than these bruises. Even though I came in last place, I still won in my heart and mind."

Each of us has our own race to run. At this very moment, some of us may find ourselves battered and bruised from stumbling over life's hurdles. The collapse of relationships, financial setbacks, the loss of loved ones, or unexpected illnesses may leave us reeling, crying out in pain as we struggle to regain our footing. Yet, despite the wounds we bear, we have the strength within us to heal. Even with our scars, it's imperative that we muster the courage to dust ourselves off and rejoin the race. No matter how difficult the journey may seem, we must press on and see it through to the end. Each step forward, no matter how small, brings us closer to the finish line, reminding us that resilience and perseverance are our greatest allies on the path to victory.

A Champion's Creed to Opposing Failure

"Champions do not become champions when they win the event, but in the hours, weeks, months and years they spend preparing for it. The victorious performance itself is merely the demonstration of their championship character."

-T. Alan Armstrong

Fighting against failure is an ongoing struggle. Every day brings forth fresh challenges that threaten to derail our pursuit of happiness. At any given moment, we may find ourselves confronted with situations that leave us feeling hopeless, disheartened, and exposed. Yet, in the face of adversity, we must persevere.

Champions live by a creed—a set of principles that guide their actions and shape their destinies. It's crucial that we embrace this creed and make it our own. By doing so, we step into our rightful roles as champions of our own lives.

I, _____, hereby agree to commit to rebuilding and restoring happiness in my life. To turn my life around, I know I must do the following:

1. _____

2. _____

3. _____

4. _____

5. _____

6. _____

7. _____

I shall continue to move through my times of trouble until I have achieved my end result. As a champion, I am making the choice to rebuild and restore my life as I desire because I deserve it. I will not let adversity stop me!

Printed name:_____

Date:_____

Signed name:_____

Date:_____

Chapter 4
Use the Power of Negative Emotions for Positive Action

"People don't ask for facts in making up their minds. They would rather have one good, soul-satisfying emotion than a dozen facts."

-Robert Keith Leavitt

In our efforts to resist failure, we often encounter reminders of the negative emotions associated with our past or present circumstances. Sadly, many of us succumb to these emotions and engage in destructive behaviors, even after committing to moving forward. This happens because we haven't yet identified positive outlets through which we can channel this intense, negative energy.

~ I found myself drifting further and further away, enveloped in a cloak of loneliness. As a recently divorced and financially struggling young man burdened by a history of abuse and financial setbacks, I couldn't shake the feeling of unworthiness. A string of failed relationships and business ventures only served to deepen my sense of hopelessness.

Gradually, that hopelessness morphed into resentment, and resentment gave way to anger. Before I knew it, anger had become my constant companion, whispering in my ear that happiness was nothing but a distant dream. Lost in a haze of bitterness, I began to view the women I dated as mere objects of desire rather than the queens they truly were. Similarly, instead of using my earnings to invest in a brighter future, I squandered them away in futile attempts to escape my troubles through gambling.

With each setback, I found myself sinking deeper into a downward spiral of negativity. Instead of using these challenges as opportunities for growth, I used them as excuses to indulge in destructive behaviors. I became trapped in a cycle of self-sabotage, blind to the extent of the damage I was inflicting upon myself.

It wasn't until much later that I realized the true toll that my anguish had taken on my well-being. In allowing myself to be consumed by bitterness and despair, I had unwittingly allowed my life to unravel before my eyes.

Numerous sources—from books and therapists to business professionals and speakers—advocate for approaching adversity and setbacks with a positive mindset. They urge us to shift our focus away from the frustrations and difficulties and cling to the hope of brighter days ahead. We're encouraged to tune out the naysayers and disregard negative influences, embracing the belief that even in the face of destitution and loss, there is a promise of eventual relief.

However, is it realistic to always maintain a positive outlook? The answer is likely no.

The Destruction of Negative Emotions

"Anger may be kindled in the noblest breasts: but in these slow droppings of an unforgiving temper never takes the shape of consistency of enduring hatred!"

-G. S. Hillard

As emotional beings, it's challenging to maintain a positive mental attitude every moment of our lives. When we experience loss or face adversity, it's natural for us to struggle to find the silver lining immediately. While some of us may attempt to seek out the positive aspects, others may resort to coping mechanisms that may not be healthy or may even harm ourselves or others.

~ A hard day at work has come to an end for Donovan, the executive director of a prestigious consulting firm. As the father of three boys and a devoted husband to his beautiful wife, Navia, he is keenly aware of the strains his long working hours have put on his family. As an acknowledgment of her support, Donovan decides to surprise his wife with long-stemmed orange roses and dinner reservations at her favorite restaurant.

Donovan enters his home. Surprisingly, darkness greets him. His boys are nowhere to be found. "Honey," he says softly. "Boys?"

Chuckling and muffled talking from upstairs catches his attention. He tiptoes toward the familiar voices of a man and woman. As he approaches the slightly opened bedroom door, his eyes widen at the unimaginable sight before him.

Donovan is overcome with hurt and anger as he watches his wife and brother toil together naked in his bed. Two of the people he has trusted more than anyone else in life have pierced his heart with the dagger of deception. Trapped between

73

thoughts of killing the two or leaving the house, he chooses the latter.

Sitting in a nearby bar, Donovan chugs his sixth rum and cola. Severely intoxicated, he drives home drunkenly and parks the car on the side of the street. Tears streaming from his eyes, he retrieves a photo of himself and his wife from his wallet. Overcome with rage, he opens the glove compartment and reaches for his .45 caliber. On a napkin, he writes, "You and my brother may now love each other with the peace of knowing you caused this." He closes his eyes and squeezes the trigger.

When under the duress of intense, negative emotions, we may engage in activities and behaviors outside of our normal character. If uncontrolled or not redirected for more productive outcomes, our distraught feelings will drive us to the brink of self-destruction or bring out our "Mr. Hyde."

Acknowledging Our "Hyde"

"All human beings... are commingled out of good and evil."

-Robert Louis Stevenson

During my time as a student in grade school, I found myself captivated by Robert Louis Stevenson's "The Strange Case of Dr. Jekyll and Mr. Hyde." This gripping tale vividly depicts the dichotomy of human nature, showcasing the dual personalities of good and evil that reside within each of us. At any given moment, our inner struggles and afflictions can lead us down paths of destructive behavior, leaving us feeling disconnected from our own identities. Here's a brief overview of the story.

~ Dr. Jekyll presents himself as a friendly, sociable, and sincere individual who is deeply committed to improving humanity. However, consumed by the belief that every person harbors both virtuous and malevolent qualities, he embarks on a perilous experiment. Driven by this obsession, he concocts a potion designed to unleash his inner, malevolent self—Mr. Hyde.

Mr. Hyde emerges as a grotesque and disfigured figure devoid of any semblance of kindness or compassion. His sole purpose is to wreak havoc and sow destruction wherever he goes. With a chilling demeanor and a relentless thirst for chaos, he ruthlessly crushes anyone who dares to stand in his way.

Beneath the surface of our outward personas—our smiles, sentimental expressions, and portrayals of success—lies another aspect of ourselves, a deeper, more primal side often hidden from view: our "Mr. Hyde." This dormant self only emerges when stirred by potent emotional elixirs such as disappointment, anger, or profound hurt, disrupting our inner peace and contentment.

It's remarkable how many individuals adamantly declare, "I could never do that," or "I would never find myself in such a situation." However, these assertions often crumble when faced with circumstances that expose our darker impulses. Consider the case of Donovan—a man seemingly living the dream with a happy marriage, three children, and a fulfilling career. The idea of contemplating suicide likely never crossed his mind until he was overwhelmed by hurt and consumed by rage, driving him to commit the unthinkable.

The Destructive Power of Misdirected Negative Emotions

"The strangest and most fantastic fact about negative emotions is that people actually worship them."

-P. D. Ouspensky

Our negative emotions can serve as either tools for reconstruction or as demolition crews, depending on how we choose to wield them. This underscores the importance of the fundamental principle of choice. When faced with negative emotions, we have the power to decide whether to channel them constructively or destructively.

Consider how productive and empowered you feel when experiencing happiness, love, and fulfillment. In these moments, it seems as though there is no obstacle too great to overcome. Positive emotions propel us forward as unstoppable forces of progress, productivity, and purpose. They empower us to turn our visions into reality and our dreams into tangible achievements.

However, when these positive emotional states are disrupted by unexpected challenges or adversity, we may find ourselves making decisions that undermine our well-being and goals. Negative emotions have the capacity to halt our progress, causing us to abandon our aspirations and withdraw from our responsibilities and relationships. Instead of building, envisioning, and providing, we may embark on destructive paths that numb us to our challenges and blind us to our potential.

It's crucial that we harness these negative emotions as catalysts for growth and transformation rather than allowing them to derail us. By facing our challenges head-on and confronting our emotions with resilience and courage, we can use them as springboards to propel us closer to our desires and aspirations.

Using the Power of Negative Emotions for Positive Action

"Behave so the aroma of your actions may enhance the general sweetness of the atmosphere."

-Henry David Thoreau

When faced with negative emotions, we often resort to destructive outlets due to a lack of proper conditioning. Throughout our lives, we tend to model our behavior after those who have a significant influence on us. Whether consciously or subconsciously, we mimic the actions of these influential figures, regardless of whether they are right or wrong. To break free from this pattern, we must recondition ourselves to harness the power of negative emotions for positive actions.

~ She had a desire to be a great novelist. As a single mother who battled depression and poverty, this poor woman didn't know how she would ever reach her dream. However, upon completing her fictitious masterpiece, she faced a greater level of sorrow. Many publishers rejected the manuscript on which she diligently worked. Rather than giving in to anger, she grabbed onto the coattail of perseverance and continued to believe in her vision. As a result, she (J.K. Rowling) published one of the most recognized pieces of contemporary fiction ever: *Harry Potter and the Philosopher's Stone.*

Mastering the skill of harnessing negative emotions for positive actions requires consistent practice and effort. It's important to continuously seek out alternative ways to channel our adverse emotions and feelings of discomfort. Adopting this concept can be particularly challenging for many individuals.

When we perceive injustice or unfair treatment, our natural response often involves feelings of hostility and a desire to retaliate. Our minds become fixated on seeking revenge or pursuing justice.

To redirect our negative emotions, we must direct ourselves to getting CLEAR.

CLEAR is an acronym for a mnemonic method designed to assist in managing anger, hurt, and resentment. It consists of five steps that can be employed when feeling overwhelmed by negative emotions: *consider, look, empty, appreciate,* and *read*.

Consider: God has endowed us with the faculties of reason, rationality, and logic, commonly referred to as common sense. However, despite possessing these attributes, negative emotions tend to override our rational thinking and lead us to behave inappropriately. Instead of resorting to harmful coping mechanisms such as excessive drinking, engaging in meaningless sexual activities, isolating ourselves, or causing harm to ourselves or others, it's essential to explore alternative ways to channel this energy.

Before succumbing to destructive impulses, we should pause and consider how we can utilize our pain to facilitate the restoration of our lives. By reframing our perspective and asking ourselves, "How can I harness this pain to bring about positive change?" we can set ourselves on a path toward healing and renewal. It's crucial to weigh the potential consequences of our actions and recognize the impact they may have on our well-being and the well-being of those around us. Through thoughtful reflection and mindful decision-making, we can steer ourselves toward the fulfillment of our aspirations and desires.

Look: The phrase "Seek and you shall find" has endured through the ages, emphasizing the importance of keeping our eyes open to opportunities. Negative emotions often obscure our vision, preventing us from recognizing the potential for personal growth and restoration. When consumed by these emotions, our focus narrows to a self-centered perspective, leading to impulsive and unproductive thoughts.

Like the concept of *consider*, seeking requires us to look beyond the immediate challenges we face. While navigating through periods of grief and adversity, it's crucial not to squander this time by assigning blame either to ourselves or to others involved in our painful experiences. Instead, we must actively seek opportunities for growth and healing.

When looking ahead feels daunting, turning to a higher power for guidance can provide solace and direction. By lifting our gaze toward the heavens, we open ourselves to divine guidance and wisdom.

Empty: Just as filled garbage cans must be emptied from the house to maintain cleanliness, negative thoughts need to be expelled from our minds and bodies in order for us to progress. Unfortunately, instead of properly disposing of this "garbage," we often unload it onto others, creating a toxic environment in our thoughts, behaviors, and attitudes. This accumulation of negativity can repel those who wish to support us in restoring our happiness and achieving our goals.

To effectively rid ourselves of this mental clutter, we can utilize an *alternative actions list*. This tool enables us to identify the activities we typically engage in when consumed by negative emotions and provides us with more positive alternatives to pursue instead. By actively replacing destructive behaviors with constructive actions, we can create a healthier and more fulfilling mindset. Here's my list as an example:

Usual action	*Alternative action*
Have sex	*Write in my book*
Get drunk	*Cook a nice dinner*
Fight, yell, argue	*Write a letter about how I feel*
Go to a nightclub	*Read a book*
Alienate myself	*Spend time with friends, family*
Waddle in pity	*Take a walk in the park or beach*
Blame others	*Play basketball, ping-pong*

Crafting an alternative action list empowers you to redirect negative emotions toward positive and life-affirming activities. We're familiar with the havoc that ensues when we allow our emotions to spiral out of control. To progress, it's essential to have alternative actions at our disposal, guiding us toward the outcomes we truly seek.

Appreciate: During times of adversity, it's common to struggle with feelings of appreciation toward anything or anyone. Our emotions often prevent us from appreciating the growth that can emerge from our pain because we fail to understand the underlying reasons for our suffering. However, attempting to comprehend circumstances beyond our control and the actions of others can impede our ability to recognize the valuable lessons that accompany hardship.

If you find yourself grappling with the concept of "understanding," remember this: you are preparing for a purpose greater than your challenges. While this realization may not immediately alleviate your suffering, embracing the turmoil in your life can expedite the healing process more effectively than continually seeking understanding. Life's complexities often defy the logic of our human minds.

Read: Finding inspiration in the victories of others after enduring suffering can be incredibly uplifting. As human beings, we are all interconnected by the complexities of life. In Ecclesiastes 1:9, Solomon reminds us that "there is no new thing under the sun," suggesting that the challenges and suffering we face today have been encountered and overcome by others before us. Exploring the works of individuals whose experiences resonate with our own can help us recognize the courage needed to progress.

Continuously dwelling on past events that led to emotional turmoil, whether caused by our own actions or those of others, serves no constructive purpose. Instead, it's essential to forgive ourselves and those who have harmed us.

Once we have forgiven, turning our attention to uplifting and empowering literature can nourish our spirits. Books that focus on preparing our minds for brighter futures and written by authors with whom we can identify can inspire us to move closer to our desired lives. The stories of others have the power to propel us to greater heights and distances than we ever imagined possible.

As previously discussed, using the power of negative emotions for positive action takes ongoing practice. Yet, it's common to occasionally forget a step or two of the CLEAR technique, as old habits often lead to inappropriate responses. In moments when you may revert to unproductive methods, it's crucial to remember to refocus and apply the CLEAR technique once again.

Chapter 5
Reject Doubt

"When in doubt, do the courageous things!"

-Jan Smuts

Life frequently underestimates our capacity to overcome its discouraging and spiritually draining blows. Currently, many of us feel disheartened because we continue to project future outcomes based on our past failures. It's essential to have faith in our ability to overcome these setbacks and transform ourselves into individuals of significant value.

~ The cool breeze of the night welcomes me as I stare wondrously at the resting lake. Waves crash gently against the rocks below. Standing against the gate, I close my eyes, inhaling deeply. The intoxicating scent of possibility fills my lungs, filtering out the nauseating smell of reality. I'm imagining a life of joy, embracing happiness in my arms. She smiles and urges me to write masterpieces as I take a seat underneath the sycamore, which is wearing the tattoos of couples' names from past generations. The pains of yesterday had finally become small scars and tiny reminders of what I had overcome. I smile.

Upon opening my eyes, I realize the unchanged climate of hurt and suffering. I remain unfulfilled and unhappy. A storm of questions suddenly rushes through my mind. *Can I really overcome this divorce and find love again? Can I really recover from this financial loss? Can I truly overcome the abuse I experienced as a child and live with a certain level of normalcy? Can I really...?*

Previous setbacks had left me hesitant to affirm any positive outcomes to the doubts swirling in my mind. The prospect of happiness seemed elusive, and my motivation waned as I dwelled on reasons for potential failure. One evening, consumed by self-doubt, I sat on the couch idly flipping through TV channels. Suddenly, something extraordinary grabbed my attention, jolting me out of my funk. I felt a wave of self-disgust for my wallowing and helplessness. Watching the program, I was struck by a realization of my own fortune and the absurdity of remaining trapped in a victim mentality. It was a turning point that spurred me to reassess my perspective and embrace gratitude for the blessings in my life.

~ He steps onto the stage with an air of confidence, towering and poised. His smile rivals the brilliance of the stage lights beaming down on him. As though untouched by any adversity, he confidently makes his way to the drum set, filling the audience, including myself, with anticipation, hoping for his success.

Without a hint of hesitation, he takes his seat and nods with determination. I watch intently as he effortlessly maneuvers the drumsticks through his wristbands. Mesmerized by his impeccable performance, I find myself bobbing my head to the rhythm. When he concludes, I join the crowd in rising to our feet, offering Dan Caro, the courageous young talent, a thunderous standing ovation.

At just two years old, Dan experienced a tragic accident that left him severely burned, resulting in the loss of his right hand and severe scarring on his left. Despite these challenges, he embodies the resilience of living with purpose. Over the years, he has found joy and purpose as a musician and professional speaker, defying the limitations imposed by his physical condition. Dan's powerful quote, "You are your limit," deeply resonates with me, motivating me to overcome doubt and pursue the fulfilling life I deserve.

Understanding Doubt

"There is nothing more dreadful than the habit of doubt. Doubt separates people. It is a poison that disintegrates friendships and breaks up pleasant relations. It is a thorn that irritates and hurts; it is a sword that kills."

-Buddha

Doubt, resembling a poisonous snake, infiltrates our minds, injecting its toxic venom into our thoughts of possibility. Its vicious attack paralyzes our ambitions, hopes, and desires, leaving us vulnerable to failure and consumed by fear. Those afflicted by doubt often experience the following symptoms:

- Excessive use of alibis or excuses
- Indecisiveness
- Lack of self-confidence
- Inability to restate a life's purpose with meaning
- Avoidance of challenges and obstacles

- Feelings of inferiority

- Fear of trying again

Despite its profound impact on us, doubt is a mental state that we can conquer. However, to do so, we must first comprehend its origins.

First Origin of Doubt *(Adverse Childhood Experiences)*

"The world is wide, and I will not waste my life in friction when it could be turned into momentum."

-Frances Willard

Many of us are unaware that a significant portion of our doubts can be traced back to adverse childhood experiences. During our formative years, when confidence is nurtured through positive interactions and support from loved ones, some of us were instead exposed to negative environments. Whether through hurtful comments like "You'll never amount to anything!" or witnessing or experiencing abuse, these early experiences can lead to deep-seated insecurities that persist into adulthood.

The scars left by childhood abuse, whether physical or emotional, can have lasting effects, undermining our belief in our own capacity for happiness and success. Despite the passage of time, these painful memories remain potent, hindering our ability to pursue the life we truly desire.

~ Cryssa's father constantly criticized her for not meeting his high expectations. Whether it was her performance on the softball field or her academic achievements, she always fell short in his eyes. His relentless disapproval left her feeling inadequate and unable to live up to his standards.

As an adult, Cryssa had the opportunity to advance her career and become an executive manager in her firm. She possessed all the necessary qualities to excel in this role—hard work, sincerity, focus, commitment, and determination. Her colleagues and superiors recognized her potential and considered her irreplaceable. However, Cryssa's past experiences haunted her, and she couldn't shake off the voice of her father telling her she wasn't good enough. Instead of seizing the opportunity, she allowed her childhood 'failures' to hold her back, ultimately declining the offer.

When past afflictions dictate your life, you miss out on opportunities for happiness and success. Despite what others may have said or done, the opportunities that come your way are tailored for you. Don't let psychological barriers from the past hinder your progress. To overcome these obstacles, recognize your true potential and greatness.

For those haunted by hurtful experiences, remember your inherent worth. Regardless of others' opinions, you are valuable, amazing, and incredible. Choose to pursue happiness actively rather than merely existing. You have the freedom to shape your life positively or carry the burdens of the past. It's time to let go of that weight and embrace a brighter future. Overcoming the scars of my stepfather's abuse and relentless criticism was a journey that spanned many years. His violent beatings and demeaning words echoed in my mind, haunting me wherever I went. I felt trapped under the weight of my abusive past, constantly reminded of my stepfather's predictions that I would amount to nothing in life.

Despite the darkness of my past, I reached a pivotal moment where I had to make a choice: continue to dwell in the shadows of my trauma or step into the light of my destiny. I decided to turn my pursuit of happiness into a personal mission—a game, if you will—of proving my stepfather wrong. I was determined to win, to show him and anyone else who doubted me that I was capable of success and happiness

By adopting this mindset of proving "him" wrong, I tapped into an inner strength that propelled me forward. I refused to let the winds of past adversity hold me back. Instead, I became an unstoppable force fueled by the desire to defy those who had once undermined my worth and potential, accomplishing each personal and professional goal. I urge you to do the same.

No matter the extent of our childhood afflictions, we all have the power to rewrite our stories and forge a path toward fulfillment. It starts with a decision—a decision to prove those who doubted you wrong and to reclaim your own happiness and success. And, as the great Eric Thomas once stated, "You owe you!"

Second Origin of Doubt (*Too many defeats*)

> *"Doubt is a pain too lonely to know that faith is his twin brother."*

> ### -Kahlil Gibran

Our doubts can also stem from experiencing repeated setbacks and failures. Whether it's in matters of love, finances, health, or any other aspect of life, facing constant disappointment can gradually erode our confidence and motivation. Each unsuccessful attempt chips away at our resolve, leaving us feeling disheartened and weary.

The vicious cycle of trying and failing can lead to a sense of agitation and dissatisfaction, making it increasingly difficult to summon the courage to try again. As our confidence wanes, the thought of embarking on another attempt becomes daunting, and we may find ourselves hesitant to take any further action.

~ David dedicated much of his life to shielding his family from the poverty he endured during his own childhood. Eager to achieve financial independence, he repeatedly invested in "get-rich-quick" schemes and the ambitious ventures of his acquaintances. Unfortunately, each investment proved fruitless, leaving him burdened with maxed-out credit cards and drained savings.

Despite years of striving to improve his financial condition, David found himself trapped in a cycle of financial struggle reminiscent of his upbringing. Instead of seeking guidance from a mentor or devising a feasible financial plan, he settled for a job that could never cover his mounting debts. Eventually, he reluctantly filed for bankruptcy as a means of escaping his financial hardships, leaving his financial dreams unfulfilled.

When faced with repeated setbacks, it's natural to feel weary and discouraged, leading us to question the point of continuing our efforts. Thoughts like "Why bother trying when nothing goes as planned?" or "Is happiness even achievable given my circumstances?" start to dominate our minds. Rather than persisting in pursuit of our goals, we resign ourselves to our current situation, believing that change is beyond reach.

In this defeated mindset, we often view those who have achieved the life we desire as lucky or favored. However, this may not be the case. It's possible that they succeeded because they refused to succumb to adversity as we did. They might have learned to use their past failures as steppingstones toward the fulfilling lives they now enjoy.

The Legendary Tale of Envious Bernard

"Envy is the art of counting the other fellow's blessings instead of your own!"

-Harold Coffin

When we abandon our pursuit of the life we desire, it's common to become fixated on someone else's success. Jealousy and envy can consume us, plunging us deeper into depression. But should we envy those who continue to strive for their goals? Absolutely not. If we do, we'll be no different from Bernard.

~ Bernard, a hardworking Kodak bear, lives next door to Jasper, a gorilla and entrepreneur. Each morning, Bernard leaves his modest home, hops into his '87 pickup truck, and heads to the warehouse, where he supervises a team of six workers.

As he sweats from helping his team unload trucks, Bernard can't help but think about Jasper. "How does someone work only a few hours a day and still afford a nice house, a fancy car, and frequently travels?" he wonders.

Upon returning home and dropping his work bag, Bernard trudges into the kitchen and grabs a beer. Sinking into his worn leather recliner, he picks up the phone and dials Jasper's number.

"Hello," Jasper answers.

"Hey Jasper, it's Bernie."

"Well—hell, howdy neighbor," Jaspers responds.

"Say, do you have a minute?" Bernard asks.

"Sure, what's on your mind?"

"I'd like it if you'd come over," Bernard says.

"Now?"

"Yes!"

Within moments, Jasper beats on the door. Bernard invites him in and greets him with a smile and cold beer. The two take a seat in the living room.

"So, what's on your mind?" Jasper asks, gulping from the chilled beer can.

"Just can't figure it out!" Bernard says, his lips in a smirk.

"What is it, Bernie?"

"You have a magnificent home, drive one of the most expensive cars in town, and take trips whenever you desire. What's your secret?"

Jaspers lounges back in the chair with a smile.

"What you see are the results of many years of struggle," Jasper grins.

"What do you mean, struggle? I don't think you know what struggling is," Bernard chuckles.

"Oh, and why not?"

"A man can only struggle for so long before he accepts defeat and settles with just being happy to be alive!"

"Not sure that I follow you," Jasper says as he sits up. "Let me share something with you."

"Go ahead," Bernard responds, taking a sip of his beer.

"As an orphan, I saw nothing but poverty and sadness around me. Each day, as I went to school, I would gaze up at Mr. Hare's mansion on top of Lion Roar Hill, and I would fantasize about being wealthy. I saw myself with a nice home and expensive cars, but most importantly, giving back to the kids."

Bernard belches. Jasper beats on his chest, slightly agitated by Bernard's interruption.

Bernard apologizes and asks Jasper to continue.

"As I got older, I realized that wealth didn't come easy. I invested every dime I made into various businesses—most resulting in financial disaster. But I didn't give up. My memory of Mr. Hare's home kept me from doing so."

Bernard nods, takes another sip, and continues to listen.

"One day, as I sat on a limb of a banana tree, thinking about how much money I had lost, I was hit by a vision."

"What vision?" Bernard asks, sitting upright.

"The vision of creating healthy banana splits!"

"I see," Bernard grins. "Healthy banana splits?"

"Yes, and following the development of my secret, I convinced the gyms and health food stores to sell the delicious sugar- and fat-free banana splits that I created!"

"Huh?"

"Think about it, Bernie. Much of the health-conscious jungle loves banana splits. They don't eat them because of the sugar content that's in traditional banana splits. Now that I have eliminated the sugar phobia and created a dessert that helps burn fat, voila! I am richer than Mr. Hare!"

"Impressive," Bernard says, nodding his head, scratching the scruff on his chin. "But I wouldn't risk what I have now to invest in something that's not guaranteed. Besides, I have tried chasing my dreams before, and it cost me thousands of dollars. It was a foolish mistake that I'll never make again!"

"Well, if that's what you've decided, Bernie, then you must be happy," Jasper says with a smile. "And if you are, I'm happy for you."

Jasper looks at his watch and sets his empty beer can on the coaster.

"I'd hate to make this visit short, Bernie, but I've got to get going. Janice, the orangutan, is coming over for dinner. If you're up to it, you should come on over..."

After escorting Jasper to the door and saying goodbye, Bernard returns to his chair, pondering the moment he gave up on his vision of starting Jungle B's Fine Cuisine. "What if I didn't quit?" he sulks.

Many of us can relate to Bernard's situation. When we decide not to try again, we often look at others with envy, failing to recognize that we're disappointed in ourselves for not giving it another shot. The key difference between those who have given up and those who persevere is the level of belief they hold in themselves.

The Power of Belief

"If you can believe, all things are possible to him who believes."

-Mark 9:23 NKJV

By nature, we humans possess incredible power. If we pause to observe, we'll realize the vast potential we hold through belief. From the majestic pyramids of Africa to the invisible airwaves transmitting our conversations via cell phones, humanity has demonstrated that virtually anything is achievable through the power of belief.

Belief serves as the invisible force, the champion within us, guiding us forward on the uncertain path of life. Without belief, our visions for the future blur in the face of adversity. Yet, belief offers encouragement, whispering, "You can make it happen," even when challenges seem insurmountable. It's belief that empowers us to discard defeated attitudes and emerge victorious.

Through belief, we can transcend the pain of divorce and heartbreak, knowing that love still awaits. We can conquer financial struggles fueled by the belief that the potential for prosperity lies within us. Belief reminds us of our worth, empowering us to walk away from toxic relationships. It urges us to start rebuilding our lives now, not later, because it assures us that tapping into our inner strength makes all things possible.

In times of seemingly insurmountable obstacles, we must embrace belief, just as the Little Engine did, and press forward with unwavering faith in our abilities. Even as an adult, this is still one of my favorite stories.

~ A little steam engine had a long train of cars to pull.

She continues effortlessly until she comes to a steep hill. She attempts to pull the heavy load over the hill, but no matter how hard she tries, she cannot move the long train of cars.

She pulls, and she pulls, and puffs and puffs. She backs up and starts off again. *Choo! Choo!*

Hmmm! The cars will not go up the hill.

Temporarily defeated, she leaves her load to seek help.

Her mind set on succeeding, the little engine encounters a big, perceivably strong steam engine standing on a side track. Running alongside him, she looks up and says, "Will you help me over the hill with my train of cars? It is so long and heavy; I can't get it over."

The big steam engine looks down at the little steam engine and replies, "Don't you see that I am through my day's work? I have been rubbed and scoured ready for my next run. No, I cannot help you."

Focus unbroken, the little steam engine continues her mission and asks another big engine the same question. He replies with the same excuse as the first.

Growing tired, the little steam engine comes to a smaller engine. She reluctantly asks, "Will you help me over the hill with my train of cars? The load is so long and heavy that I can't get it over the hill."

"Yes, indeed!" says the smaller steam engine. "I'll be glad to help you if I can."

The two little engines return to the load. Together, they *puff* and *puff*, *chug* and *chug*. Slowly, the cars began moving. Pulling with all their might, the two sing:

"I think I can! I think I can! I think I can!"

They soon overcome the hill.

On a level plain, the little steam engine thanks her helper and says goodbye, continuing her journey. Filled with the feeling of accomplishment, she pulls her load and sings: "I thought I could! I thought I could! I thought I could! I thought I could!"

The cargo of depression, unhappiness, and loss are seemingly too much for us to carry up the hill toward individual restoration. Like the little engine, we only need to find a little help. Often, those who appear capable of helping us are not positioned to help in the way we desire. The little help that we need is the spark of belief that is found deep within us.

Watty Piper's *The Little Engine That Could* is a timeless children's bedtime story that illustrates the strength of a willing spirit. Many of the challenges you encounter will appear impossible to overcome at first sight. Thankfully, you can negotiate your obstacles when you execute the power of belief.

Executing Belief

"One life is all we have and we live it as we believe in living it. But to sacrifice what you are and to live without belief, that is a fate more terrible than dying."

-Joan of Arc

Harnessing the power of belief relies heavily on the state of our minds. When our minds are clouded with doubt or feelings of failure, it leaves little room for possibility and hope. Despite experiencing moments of inadequacy, it's vital to acknowledge a crucial truth: Doubt and feelings of failure are lies we've come to accept as reality, and they must be expelled from our minds.

To fully embrace the power of belief, you must first cultivate a mental environment conducive to restoration and the pursuit of happiness. This involves three essential steps: confronting our lies, removing them from our minds, and telling a new story— one of empowerment and positivity.

Confront the Lie

"The greatest deception men suffer is from their own opinions."

-Leonardo da Vinci

When we convince ourselves that success or happiness is beyond our reach or that we're insignificant, inadequate, or unworthy, we're feeding ourselves lies. Similarly, the belief that engaging in destructive, criminal, or self-damaging activities is the only way to cope with our struggles is also untrue. These lies warp our perception of reality, burying the truth deep beneath layers of past failures, adversity, and pain.

As a result of these distorted beliefs about ourselves, it's not uncommon to turn to harmful coping mechanisms such as excessive drinking, smoking, violence, or sexual aggression. These actions provide temporary relief from our suffering but ultimately perpetuate our cycle of unhappiness and dissatisfaction. Our lives become hostage to these lies, hindering us from attaining the happiness we yearn for.

To uncover the truth hidden beneath these layers of untruths, we must confront the lies that society, our past experiences, and our own minds have ingrained within us. Only by challenging these lies head-on can we begin to dismantle their hold on us and rediscover our true worth and potential.

Some of the lies that hinder our ability to move forward are:

• *We are too old to start over after losing our jobs, our relationships, our marriages, or our financial and social statuses. As a result, we do not trust ourselves to restore and rebuild our lives.*

• *Our happiness is predicated on our need to feel wanted and desired in relationships; therefore, we exert precious energy in futile circumstances instead of utilizing this energy to seek ways to strengthen our self-confidence and individuality.*

• *We are not good enough or worthy of leadership positions, and therefore, we pass on these opportunities to others.*

• *We are failures because our numerous attempts at achievement, love, or financial gain have resulted in more sorrow.*

Therefore, we remain unmotivated and unhopeful as our desires slowly dissipate.

- *Our existence is pointless, and therefore, we live without emotion or care for what we do to ourselves and to others.*

- *Our criminal past prevents us from carrying out visions of success and happiness when all we need is to use our newfound freedom to find resources that can help us rise above society's inaccurate depictions of our future.*

- *Our past hinders a brighter future of purpose, mission, and vision and, therefore, causes us to remain unimproved, discouraged, and afraid.*

The lies mentioned above have greatly diminished our drive to rebuild and find purpose in our lives. How much longer must we endure the tyranny of these untruths? Until we recognize our inherent worth and potential greatness. Until we're prepared to view ourselves in the mirror as embodiments of happiness, success, hope, and strength. Until we're ready to emerge from the depths of depression, hopelessness, doubt, and all other barriers hindering our progress. Until our determination to revitalize our lives outweighs the negative self-perceptions holding us back.

Summoning the courage to confront the lies we've embraced is essential. Some of us remain oblivious to the fact that we're living a life built on falsehoods, as we rarely entertain the idea that we could deceive ourselves. Ironically, this belief in our own honesty can itself be another lie.

Remove the Lie

"Sometimes I lie awake at night, and ask, 'Where have I gone wrong?' Then a voice says to me, 'This is going to take more than one night.'"

-Charles Schulz

Once we summon the courage to confront the lies we've been living, we must take further steps to eliminate them from our minds. Confrontation alone is not enough; we must swiftly expel these falsehoods to make room for truth. Lies and truth cannot coexist, much like night and day. To purge our minds of these toxins, we can engage in activities that promote mental clarity and embrace truth. One such method is the practice of mind sweeping.

Mind sweeping involves a range of techniques or exercises designed to eradicate lies from our minds. Like the way the military clears minefields of explosives in war-torn areas, mind sweeping requires patience and specialized methods to remove the lies that entrap us in false beliefs and identities. This approach encompasses four main techniques: prayer, Tai Chi, yoga, and mindfulness. Through these practices, you can dismantle the barriers of deception and cultivate a mindset rooted in truth.

Prayer

"Pray as though everything depended on God. Work as though everything depended on you."

-Saint Augustine

Prayer yields profound results. Countless individuals have experienced wisdom, strength, improved health, and a sense of purpose through prayer. It has transformed abusive behavior into love, healed sickness, and inspired financial success. For believers, prayer unites the mind and spirit, fostering contentment, hope, and joy. Below is an example of a prayer you can incorporate into your life:

"Dear Heavenly Father,

I come to you in a state of confusion. Help me recognize who I really am, grant me the strength to change how I see myself and my circumstances, and instill in me the vision I am to fulfill. Forgive me for the wrongs I have done to myself and others, and plant me firmly in the spiritual and mental gardens of peace. Right now, I have feelings of inadequacy, fear, hurt, loneliness, and depression. In exchange for these, I ask that you give me the spirits of peace, wisdom, and courage. Give me the power to change the conditions within my ability and help me accept the circumstances that I have no control over...In your son's Jesus name, I pray, Amen!"

Whether we call it meditation or spiritual cleansing, prayer is one of the most powerful tools we have in our arsenal for removing lies from our minds. Many of us negate prayer because we do not believe in a spiritual power greater than ourselves, or we pray for things such as financial wealth, love, optimal health, and the fulfillment of dreams and ambitions, but we do so without belief.

~ Sitting at a coffee shop in Greensboro, and after writing this piece on prayer, I notice a young gentleman staring at me. Holding a pocket-size Bible, he engages me.

"Excuse me," he says. "What church do you attend?"

As we were in Greensboro, he assumed that I attended one of the local churches.

"I attend New Jerusalem," I answer.

"Oh, I heard you speak about prayer while you were on the phone."

"Really?"

"Yes."

The barista's grinding of coffee beans in the background made it difficult to hear him.

"Do you mind sitting over here?" I ask.

"Okay," he responds and pulls up a chair. "My name is Lucian."

"Hello, Lucian," I respond with a smile, "my name is Ellard, or Ell for short."

The young man appeared to have been in his late twenties or early thirties; it was hard to tell.

"Ell," Lucian says, "I feel like I am supposed to talk with you."

"Oh," I respond surprisingly. "Why?"

"I've been praying for God to send me someone I can talk to. And when I heard you on the phone talking about the power of God and prayer, I figured you'd be the one to speak with."

I nod my head, wincing at the young man.

"Are you a pastor or a minister?" he asks.

I smile.

"I'm a servant," I respond with a smile. "What's on your mind?"

"I am struggling and don't know what to do..."

Lucian shared with me his struggles with addictions to pornography, drugs, and alcohol and how he felt trapped in confusion. He often found himself doing things he didn't want to do and living a life of aimless wandering. However, prayer became his refuge and helped him overcome these obstacles. From feeling compelled to engage in destructive behaviors to wandering without direction, Lucian described a life of discontent that seemed inescapable until he discovered the power of prayer.

"Prayer has helped me more than any counseling session ever could... I'm not completely over some of the problems in my life, but I believe I will overcome them if I continue to pray..."

As you embark on the journey to restore your happiness, prayer can serve as a powerful tool to rediscover your purpose in life. Living entails seizing the opportunities presented to you rather than being held back by circumstances or settling for mediocrity. Every setback and moment of sorrow presents an opportunity for growth and improvement. Prayer reveals the resilience you have within, demonstrating that it is stronger than any obstacle you encounter.

Tai Chi

"Mastering others is strength; mastering yourself is true power!"

-Lao-Tzu

Tai Chi is becoming more popular for people looking to feel better mentally. This gentle martial art helps reduce stress and clear your mind by connecting you with your inner self, or Qi (pronounced "chee"). Qi represents the life force coursing through the body's invisible channels, embodying the essence of life or spirit. The effectiveness of this mind-clearing method lies in deep breathing combined with deliberate, slow movements.

~ Sitting on a local park bench, infuriated about a business deal that fell apart, I watch a group of men and women performing wide-arm movements and slow-motion kicks. Graceful as ballerinas, they appear to flow with the summer zephyrs—slowly stepping forward and backward, turning, and breathing deeply. In awe, I approach a neighboring spectator.

"Do you know what they are doing?" I ask.

"They are practicing Tai Chi," the kind woman answers.

"That looks peaceful," I smile.

"It really is," she smiles back. "I teach it."

"Really? So what's the purpose of this exercise?"

"Without going too much in-depth about it," the young lady continues. "Tai Chi helps us focus on what matters most: our connection with our inner self and not on the matters of life. A conditioned spirit helps us realize that there's no such thing as bad circumstances, just negative and positive energies. When we accept negative energies, we must then allow them to flow through us until we become centered. Tai Chi has become the technique for me and countless others to remove these unwanted energies from us..."

Learning how to unlock the internal power that is released through performing Tai Chi is essential to removing lies from our minds. Taking a few moments out of our days to practice this mind-sweeping art can help us improve the quality of our lives and make us remember the great individuals that we are.

Yoga

"The mind is everything; what you think, you become."

-Buddha

When we feel good about ourselves, we see the individuals in the mirror as people of great worth. Unfortunately, many of us are still blinded because our lies have damaged our inner selves. This prevents us from seeing beyond our anguish. Through the power of yoga, we can gain the clarity we need to see ourselves as powerful, beautiful, confident, and successful.

Yoga is a powerful and beautiful art that includes a set of techniques designed to help us see beyond our limitations. We (as human beings) restrict ourselves from experiencing happiness or ideal lives because we impose our own restrictions. We must understand that it is not our environments, circumstances, or pasts that hinder us from the lives we deserve; it is the state of our minds.

~ After losing her sister in a fatal car accident, Mariah's perfect world was turned upside down. The death of her sister created an emotional divide between her parents, which pushed her to drugs and alcohol for comfort. On the brink of self-destruction, Mariah decided to attend a yoga class with her best friend. Initially uncomfortable, Mariah later became intrigued by the teachings and desired the calmness the attendees exuded. Determined to turn around her life, Mariah used the power of yoga to overcome her sorrow and regain her spiritual, physical, and mental balance. "Before experiencing the power of yoga," Mariah said, "I wanted to numb myself from the pain. I felt like a nobody when my family collapsed. Thanks to yoga, I relearned how to find myself and happiness."

The exercises and poses of yoga are to help us ascend into purity, or truth, and realize the innate divinity (Godly power) within us. Yoga teaches us that oneness with our greater self is essential to living healthier, both physically and mentally. For those of us who have different religious backgrounds, yoga does not contradict any beliefs. If anything, it helps to bring us closer to and more aligned with our inner spirituality.

Mindfulness

"Feelings come and go like clouds in a windy sky. Conscious breathing is my anchor."

-Thich Nhat Hanh

Mindfulness is a critical element to the path of mental freedom and subsequent enlightenment. This mind-sweeping technique pushes us to live in the present and to bring our mind and body into harmony. Rather than pushing us to ask the question "Why?" about our hardships, mindfulness teaches us how to find peace during our moments of anxiety and despair.

~ Following her shift at a local bar, Brenda heads to her sedan parked two streets away. As she walks toward her car, two young men in a black luxury vehicle with tinted windows watch her from a distance.

As Brenda searches for her keys, the two well-dressed young men approach her from behind. Momentarily startled, Brenda reaches into her purse and grabs her pepper spray but releases it at the charming voice of the taller of the two men.

"I hate to bother you," he says with a foreign accent, "but I wonder if you can help me."

"With what?" Brenda smiles, sensing no threat.

While the gentleman and Brenda converse, the other young man, smiling innocently, slowly motions behind the friendly belle. Suddenly, he cuffs her mouth and drags the kicking beauty into a nearby alley, where he and his friend savagely rape and brutally beat her. A transient discovers her unconscious body hours later.

"I should have died that night," Mariah cried. "Perhaps I did inside. After leaving the hospital, I stayed in my house for six months, too afraid to go anywhere, spending most of my days and nights scrubbing my body until I bled. I often pondered suicide as I found myself living to die."

"Following years of feeling worthless and scared while suffering from paralyzing anxiety attacks, I had to relearn how to live...Mindfulness meditation has helped me significantly with overcoming my unforgettable night. Whereas I would normally pop three to four anti-depressant pills, I remember my mindfulness training..."

The practice of mindfulness is most helpful and powerful when we become emotionally imbalanced. Whenever we become angry or encounter any other adverse emotion, mindfulness directs us to the path of immediate calmness and keeps us focused on living in the now and not on our past.

Any of the mind-sweeping techniques can help you remove the lies from your mind. As with anything of great worth, these techniques will require a sacrifice of time and energy. It is up to you to determine if your mental freedom is worth it.

Tell a New Story

My past is history, a tale I no longer have to live! My future, however, is full of great opportunities waiting to be written.

-Coach Ell

Once we've untangled our minds from the grip of lies using various mind-sweeping techniques, it's crucial to start rewriting our inner narrative. The old stories of failure, inadequacy, brokenness, scarcity, and despair should be cast aside permanently, making room for a new, empowering story of growth, resilience, and success.

~ Many of my colleagues and close friends were curious about how I managed to overcome the mental and physical abuse I endured in my life. They were surprised because they had heard stories of people with similar backgrounds resorting to crime, suicide, or perpetual blame and resentment. Instead of divulging my entire healing process, I simply told them that I aspired to be the "unexpected ending rarely seen in a great horror story."

Many of us have experienced, or are currently experiencing, narratives filled with loneliness, depression, and feelings of unworthiness. However, we no longer need to be confined to the destructive or unproductive roles defined by our pasts. Instead, we can seize control of the script and rewrite our stories with honesty and strength, inspiring others to do the same. Starting today, we can begin narrating tales of success, achievement, healing, deliverance, and happiness. Let me illustrate how I embarked on writing my new story.

• "Although I am divorced, I am a good man and will become a great husband."

• "Although I lost all my money in businesses, I will become wealthy through a plan involving my talents, others' wisdom, and direction from God."

• "Despite my past abuse, I am capable of loving and caring for women without treating them as sexual objects."

• "Even though I've suffered from the loss of my home, I will find the resources necessary to get a bigger home in which I will have my writing studio."

• Despite getting laid off from multiple jobs, I will devote my time and energy to developing financial freedom so I do not have to depend on Corporate America."

When we begin telling ourselves new stories, we will start performing accordingly. We will smile more and recognize ways to profit from our talents. We will lift our heads higher with confidence. We will look in the mirror and see ourselves as handsome men or beautiful women capable of experiencing love, happiness, and higher achievement. Through our new stories, we will have the power to live life with purpose and vision.

Believe in Your New Story

> *"I am whoever I believe I am!"*
>
> *-Anonymous*

Believing in our new stories is essential to leaving behind our old selves. When my stepfather told me repeatedly that I would become a homosexual man because, at 13 years old, I did not want to have sex with a prostitute, I did whatever I could to prevent this from happening, especially after I had been molested. I avoided taking showers when other boys did and eventually entered a world of promiscuity. I really believed that, as long as I didn't engage in the activities of gays (or what I thought homosexuals did), I would be okay. I wasn't okay. I had sunken deeper into an abyss of discontentment and self-destruction. Deep in my heart, I knew that this wasn't my story. I had to believe that I was meant to do more with my life. Over time, this belief helped me change my life.

Telling ourselves a new story and believing in it takes time. We'll become frustrated with moving forward because we've been conditioned to live and believe in a certain way of life. Breaking habits is difficult, and it requires courage to distance ourselves from the behaviors of the people we once were. Here's something we should consider before we refuse to believe in our new stories: Before we lived out the lies in our lives, we had to believe in them wholeheartedly. Whereas the old stories were created by others and our environments, **our new ones will be created by us**.

Unfortunately, many of us will continue living out past tales because they have become lullabies of comfort despite the inevitable and tragic endings to follow. This doesn't have to be your truth. If you're willing to put forth the effort necessary, you can change the trajectory of your life, starting today.

No More Doubt

"The moment I believe I can, I will!"

-Adon Muyro

Where there is no doubt, there are no lies to accept—just opportunities. Earlier, we looked at the origins of doubt and how to proceed in the newness of life through the power of belief, and we examined three methods to help us: *confront the lies, remove the lies*, and *tell a new story*. If you are to remember anything from this section, you should remember that you are responsible for defining who you are and how you should progress in life. You also need to remember that no one and no circumstance can make you feel inferior unless you allow it. Either you give doubt permission to keep you bound in the chains of lies, or you take the information recently discussed in this section and continue to move forward. The choice is yours.

Chapter 6
Acknowledge Your Strong Whys

"Forget about all the reasons why something may not work.
You only need to find one good reason why it will."

-Dr. Robert Anthony

In the moments when hopelessness meets us with tremendous force, we must find a way to keep moving forward. We must do so even when we feel depleted of every ounce of energy. Considering the unbearable circumstances you face, you need to remember the strong reasons behind rebuilding your life.

~ I had finally reached the end of my rope, slamming my bedroom door. Nothing appeared to be going right in my life. I had joined hundreds of others who had lost their jobs to the plummeting telecom market.

Unaware of how fast my circumstances could worsen, I was pushed into playing the "car or house" game. Each month, I had to determine if I would pay either my car loan or the mortgage. Rude and obnoxious collection calls soon flooded my voicemail and caller ID, leaving me stressed and ready to give in to defeat.

Trapped in a situation with no apparent solution, I recognized the necessity of providing a roof over my little brother's head. As a result, I chose to prioritize this over my car loan payments, allowing the repossession of my cherished vehicle. This decision plunged me into a sense of worthlessness.

One evening, drawn by the noise of the television upstairs, I left my bedroom and followed the sound of my brother's laughter. "Hey, Ellard," my youngest brother greeted me with a smile, breaking my train of thought. "Are you okay?" he asked, his innocent eyes filled with genuine concern for me.

Suppressing my tears, I gazed at my brother. He was oblivious to the financial turmoil I was going through. All he knew was that he had a home, food, and the security of never being in foster care again. In that moment, I stopped frowning. A fleeting smile crossed my face. "I'm okay," I assured him, taking a seat beside him and gently rubbing his head. "I'm okay," I repeated, finding solace in his presence.

"Are you really sure?" he asked again, leaning his head on my shoulder.

"Yes, I just have some things on my mind," I replied.

"Well," he said, looking at me with his puppy-dog brown eyes, "I want you to know that I appreciate everything you do for me. I know I haven't done everything right, but I love you very much..."

Tears filled my eyes, and my heart raced. The idea of him returning to the foster care system stirred a powerful and unexplainable determination in me. I couldn't bear to see him go back to a system that had failed to shield him from abuse and neglect. I was resolute—I had to fight relentlessly to ensure he remained housed and safe.

Over the following months, my resilience was put to the test. I took on jobs from day labor companies and worked full-time as a call center representative, despite the low pay and the temptation to quit each day. But my brother's well-being kept me pushing forward despite the challenges.

Life has a peculiar way of forcing us to make sacrifices. *"Do I keep this and give up that?" "Do I sit here waiting, or do I take a chance?"* Many of us yearn to escape from life's challenges and hide away, avoiding our responsibilities. But what does cowardice achieve? Absolutely nothing.

Even amidst your suffering, there's no need to retreat or seek temporary solace in harmful behaviors like alcohol, sex, or violence. When it feels like striving is futile, impossible, or irrelevant, remember your "strong whys."

Identifying Strong Whys

"Most people never run far enough on their first wind to find out they've got a second."

-William James

In the face of adversity, it's easy to lose sight of our motivations for pushing through tough times. Yet, despite the challenges, we owe it to ourselves to emerge like the rising sun from the depths of our struggles. We have within us the innate power to triumph and illuminate the world with our resilience.

~ For nearly three decades, Tyler dedicated his time and expertise to propel his company toward growth. Despite his extensive knowledge and commitment, he was unexpectedly shown the door, leaving him bewildered and facing financial uncertainty. Returning home to a looming foreclosure, Tyler sank into despair on his luxurious Italian-leather couch, questioning where it all went wrong and what to do next. Days turned into weeks as he languished in depression, seeking comfort in nostalgic Western reruns.

Summoning his inner strength, Tyler lifts himself from the sofa and starts packing his belongings, beginning with his desk. "Damn this!" he yells, pushing piles of papers onto the floor, tossing other unnecessary items into the wastebasket, exclaiming, "I can't believe this!"

Midway through his outburst, the thought of ending his life crosses his mind. Then, he notices a picture of his son lying on the floor, which prompts a smile. "Okay," he says, swayed by his son's enduring smile. "Okay! I understand," he says, pinning his son's picture to the wall.

Instead of staying trapped in despair, Tyler takes action. He grabs a tablet, sits on the floor, and begins drafting a plan to overcome his financial setback.

Like my brother was for me and Tyler's son was for him, strong whys can stem from anything or anyone we have deep emotional connections with. These emotional ties possess the ability to inspire faith, confidence, and the courage needed to overcome insurmountable challenges. Reflecting on your past accomplishments, you'll likely notice that many were driven by these emotional attachments. Here are some examples of strong whys you might have:

- Family
- Close friends
- Loathing for the impoverished past
- Strong desire for betterment or change

- Unsatisfactory current financial and social positions

- Strong desire for something or someone

- Burning desire to overcome adversity

- Dedication to changing and bettering the lives of others

- Strong discontent for heartaches due to loss

Each of the examples mentioned above triggers an emotional response that can fuel you when you feel too tired to continue. This raises a question: If our strong whys can drive us to succeed in times of adversity, why do some of us still fall short? The answer is logical and simple.

Weak Whys—The Imposters of Strong Whys

"It is weakness rather than wickedness which renders men unfit to be trusted with unlimited power."

-John Adams

Though *weak whys* may appear to be strong whys, they lack the emotional power to propel us forward during challenging times. As a result, they fail to provide the necessary boost when we encounter obstacles and hardships.

~ James had good intentions when he introduced me to the business opportunity he had joined while I was in my undergraduate program. He believed that this opportunity could alleviate the financial struggles I faced as a "starving" student. "Ellard," he said optimistically, "I truly believe this business will help us achieve our financial dreams!"

"Why do you think so?" I asked.

116

"I'm collaborating directly with a few individuals who have become millionaires through this business. Perhaps you should consider dropping out of school and joining me to build this business!" he suggested.

At that time in my life, a few years before my venture with Troy, I was torn between my strong desire to complete my bachelor's degree and the allure of making money.

"Okay, James," I said, momentarily enticed, "what is the investment?"

"A couple hundred dollars!"

I used money from my savings to get started with James on the business opportunity that lasted a few months. Despite attending every meeting and giving numerous presentations, I didn't see any significant financial returns. My commitment to finishing school remained my top priority, which meant I couldn't dedicate the full energy needed to succeed in that business. Therefore, I shifted my focus back to my academic desires, and a couple of years later, I successfully graduated with my degree.

Admittedly, I didn't succeed because my *why* wasn't strong enough to drive me to perform the necessary tasks for success. My dedication to finishing school outweighed my ambition to excel in the business opportunity.

Many of us are in a phase of rebuilding our lives, yet we consistently face setbacks. We aspire to improve and recognize the necessity to do so but find ourselves grappling with ongoing challenges. Frequently, we attempt to change the course of our lives, driven by weak whys. We understand logically the importance of quitting smoking and drinking, losing weight, cutting off toxic relationships, and abandoning other unhealthy habits, but we lack a strong emotional connection to these changes. Consequently, we eventually give up and settle for lifestyles that fall short of what we truly deserve.

Addressing Weak Whys

"We are not weak if we make a proper use of those means which the God of Nature has placed in our power... the battle, sir, is not to the strong alone, it is to the vigilant, the active, the brave."

-Patrick Henry

Weak whys lack the depth and emotional drive necessary to sustain our commitment. They are fleeting thoughts, intentions, or ideas about personal achievement that may sound appealing initially but fail to keep us fully dedicated. When driven by weak whys, our mindset tends to be: *"I can achieve this goal as long as everything goes smoothly."* However, as we've experienced, life often throws unexpected challenges our way. In those difficult and emotionally draining moments, weak whys provide little support. They don't offer the strength or hope needed to navigate through adversity like our strong whys provide.

~ As I led a leadership conference for college students, I posed a question to the attentive and discerning group: "Are there any goals you've set out to achieve but didn't? And if so, why not?"

The group looked at me with blank expressions, and I patiently waited. Eventually, a young lady raised her hand.

"Yes, there are! I'm almost embarrassed to say this," she said, looking around at her peers. "I didn't achieve many of my goals or obligations because I failed to remain committed."

"Failed to commit?" I asked.

"Yes, they eventually didn't seem so important," she continued, smiling.

Another young lady chimed in, "Sometimes, I realize that there are other things I'd rather do instead..."

The room suddenly burst with excuses for leaving obligations unfulfilled. The following are a few that we, too, may have used in the past or currently use today:

- "There are too many distractions!"

- "It's too painful!"

- "I get too overwhelmed!"

- "My life is too hectic!"

- "I didn't see a point!"

- "I realized that it's not that important!"

Weak whys breed excuses. Excuses hinder our progress toward achieving contentment and happiness. They discourage us from persevering and fighting for what we want. When we choose to give up the fight, it fuels feelings of despair and anguish.

Relying on weak motivations to drive us toward happiness and success is a recipe for disaster. Now, let's continue with the story.

The laughter in the group persisted as students began pointing out each other's failure to fulfill their obligations. I found myself chuckling at some of the excuses being shared.

"I have a question," I said, silencing the energetic crowd. "All of you have achieved some level of success in your life, would you agree?"

The crowd nodded.

"So, what's the difference between the goals you've achieved in the past and the ones you've let fall by the wayside?"

Smiles appeared on all their faces.

"Many of the goals I achieved," a young man spoke, "gave me a sense of accomplishment. The feeling of achievement far outweighed the sacrifices and effort I had to give!"

"Based on what you just said," I said, rubbing my chin, "you fulfilled certain desires because they gave you *emotional* satisfaction?"

"Yes," he answered.

"That's the same with me," blurted another young lady. "If I am passionate or emotionally charged to do something, I will do whatever it takes to make it happen..."

For the rest of the conference, we delved into the distinctions between strong whys and weak whys. This discussion provided the group with a fresh perspective on their desires, aspirations, and objectives.

While weak whys may impede your ability to excel in challenging circumstances, strong whys will propel you far beyond your perceived limitations. They will help you achieve your dreams and aspirations, even when circumstances seem insurmountable. Armed with strong whys, you can overcome every obstacle that threatens your happiness and desired outcomes.

Jot Down Your Strong Whys

"I can't change the direction of the wind, but I can adjust my sails to always reach my destination."

-Jimmy Dean

Suffering and pain have the power to make us lose sight of why we're fighting. When we cease striving for the happiness we desire, it's akin to accepting defeat—the death of our dreams, desires, hopes for the future, and our sense of purpose. Consequently, we're left feeling burdened by despair and anguish. To prevent this, it's essential to document our strong motivations. I learned this valuable lesson from Mrs. Rose, a wise elderly woman I encountered while volunteering at a convalescent center.

"Good afternoon," I greet, standing in the doorway.

Mrs. Rose raises her head from her notebook and meets my eyes with her gentle gaze.

"Hello dear," she says with a smile.

"What are you doing?" I ask as I walk over to her bed.

"Oh, nothing, hon. Just writing."

As I sit beside her bed, a wave of sadness washes over me as I watch Mrs. Rose struggle to sit up.

"When you live long enough," she says, "the body reminds us that youth is but a fleeting memory."

"I see," I chuckle, looking down at her notebook. "What are you writing?"

She smiles warmly and closes her eyes.

"Child, I'm writing down all the good memories I have," she says, "and the reasons why I must keep fighting this illness."

She opens her eyes and turns to me.

"Would you like to see my list of reasons that keep me in the good fight?" she continues.

"Sure."

I gently take the notebook from Mrs. Rose's trembling yet soft and aged hands. Inside, there are two lists: "Good Memories" on the left and "My Reasons to Fight" on the right. The list titled "My Reasons to Fight" catches my attention.

- ❖ My daughter
- ❖ My church
- ❖ My grandchildren
- ❖ My love for living
- ❖ My assignment
- ❖ My friends
- ❖ Family dinners
- ❖ ***Homemade chili***

"Homemade chili?" I chuckle.

"Child, yes," she grins. "It's to *live* for!"

We both laugh.

"Young man," she says softly.

"Yes, ma'am."

"Would you like to know why I have this list?" she asks, her eyes glistening with hope.

"Yes."

"I'm aware that this illness may claim my body," she says, "but it'll never claim my life."

"Excuse me?" I say, a little confused.

"This list," she says, turning her attention to the notebook, "is a record of my actual life—not this sickness. The moments that have made me smile and the reasons I made it through my troubles are what made living life so great. There's already too much negativity in this world that robs people of their happiness and joy. This list helps me to remember the pleasantries that life has offered me. And don't get me started about that man of mine. Boy, Clarence could sing the Blues like nobody's business."

Reflecting on my own reasons for living, I remain attentive to the wisdom of the elderly woman.

"Until God says it's over," she continues, "I must continue to fight. And if it is my time to leave, at least I know that my eight decades on this Earth meant something. And when I do leave, I know Clarence will welcome me into his strong arms again."

Mrs. Rose turns to me, her eyes demanding me to sit upright.

"Young man," she begins to cry. "I want you to make me a promise."

"Anything, Mrs. Rose."

"Never forget your smiles and the reasons you must keep fighting. Hard times will steal these gifts from you if you let them. Promise me that you'll keep on fighting because you're fighting to smile more than you frown..."

Mrs. Rose taught me so much about life and purpose. Her determination and zeal to live inspired me more than she would've ever known. She was a bright day to my calamitous moments. I was heartbroken when I learned that she passed away two weeks later. One of the nurses told me that she died peacefully with a smile and left a letter for me.

Mr. Thomas, you have been a pleasure. You're a kind and gentle young man, one I feel has been here before. Thank you for sharing your deepest sorrows with me. I've prayed for you each day, asking God to grant you the peace and strength you need to carry the burden you've been carrying. If you're reading this, that means our time has come to its undelightful end, but I ask you to do me a favor. Find love when you can. Seek truth through the Divine always, and never put your destiny in the hands of anyone else. You're a remarkable young man, and I believe we'll speak once again in God's palace. Continue to move forward and live a life worth living.

Your dear ol' friend,

Bethel Rose

Due to the challenges I encountered in my life, I came close to breaking the promise I made to Mrs. Rose. Strangely, I didn't recall her wise words until I made the decision to write this book.

Jotting down your strong whys and placing them in plain sight will help you remember the important reasons for moving forward and fighting through your difficult times. Also, they'll give you a new perspective on your situations during the dreary moments that often summon defeat, discontentment, and fear.

Even when life shows us its darkest sides, we possess the ability to transcend the peaks of despair and failure, thanks to the strength of our strong whys. As Mrs. Rose suggested, this power lies in documenting our purposes or strong motivations, guiding us along the path to happiness.

For those of us who have lost sight of our strong whys, now is the perfect time to list the people, words, memories, or visions that will propel us forward. Before putting pen to paper, it's crucial to ensure that these motivating factors evoke strong emotional connections. Once you've written them down, place the list somewhere visible where you'll read it every day.

Strong Whys list

1. _____

2. _____

3. _____

4. _____

5. _____

6. _____

7. _____

8. _____

9. _____

10. _____

Before succumbing to fatigue or any other physically and mentally debilitating obstacles that often immobilize others, we must draw upon our strong whys for strength and press onward. Without these motivating factors, you cannot achieve the success and happiness you rightfully deserve.

Chapter 7
Get Back Up Again

"What lies behind you and what lies in front of you, pales in comparison to what lies inside of you."

-Ralph Waldo Emerson

The crushing weight of sorrow can bring us submissively to our knees, impeding our ability to rise again. Yet, considering our stress, we still can prevail. *We can get back up again.*

~ I remember watching my youngest brother and sister, Eddie and Betty, attempting to walk for the first time. They were innocent and full of zeal—courageous even. They didn't worry about hitting their heads on the nearby coffee table or even falling on the burnt orange shagged carpet. Imminent danger surrounded them, but these kids were fearless. They had only one goal in mind: get to our mother on the other side of the living room.

Wobbling left and right, they pattered toward their mark, falling within a few feet of starting and sometimes within a few feet of my mother. Each time they fell, my sister Shameka and I would bring them back to the starting point. Fatigue eventually set in their little, pudgy legs. Feeling momentarily defeated, they whined when we tried to have them begin again for the twentieth time. After numerous defeats, their vision became clouded.

"Mom," I laughed. "They've had enough!"

"They can do it," my mother uttered. "Come to Mommy!"

Betty stopped crying and squirmed until Shameka released her. Eddie, on the other hand, looked up at me with his tear-filled eyes and buried his head into my chest. Shameka steadied the little one on her feet. Eyes focused on my mother, she wobbled a few steps to the left and fell hard. Surprisingly, she didn't cry. Instead, she crawled back to the starting line. Once again, Shameka lifted her upright; Betty darted forward, sliding face-first into the carpet.

"Okay," Shameka said, "I think she's had enough!"

"You think?" I chuckled, shaking my head.

"She can do it," my mother encouraged the nine-month-old contender. "Shameka, start her over again!"

Shameka helps the relentless, determined child to her feet. I continue to shake my head, thinking how pointless this was. Once Shameka lets go of Betty's little hands, she takes off. We all watch as she stumbles to the right, stopping and regaining her balance. Taking another step, she squats as if she's ready to call it quits. Suddenly, she stands erect, never losing sight of my mother and her welcoming arms. She takes one more step, nearly tripping over her foot, but doesn't fall. With only a few more steps to take, she springs and collapses in my mother's arms, giggling triumphantly.

Eddie sees his five-minute-younger sister in the champion's circle. He kicks and squirms. Setting him upright on the floor, I hold his hands. He anxiously steps off before I can let go. He crashes onto his bottom, diaper first.

"Come to Mommy," my mother smiles, her arms open wide.

Eddie falls a few more times. I had given up on the poor sap. I believe he did too, that is, until he looks at his sister. Her grunts and other cute baby noises must have meant, "If I can do it, you can too, Eddie." Without warning, or as much as a sound, Eddie dashes from my hands and doesn't stop until he arrives safely into my mother's arms.

As adults, have we forgotten our fearless youth or our toddler courage? In the past, we all have experienced the effects of falling, but we somehow stood up again. Beat up and bruised, scarred and scratched, we probably cried or whined, but we refused to stay down. The way we face our current challenges shouldn't be any different.

To lift ourselves out of depression and into a state of happiness, perhaps we should consider calling upon the courageous children we once were. Maybe those children can offer us insight and remind us of our innate determination to rise again.

The Fall is Real

"Our greatest glory consists not in never failing but in rising every time we fall."

-Oliver Goldsmith

During the 1980s and 1990s, a well-known catchphrase was featured in a commercial for a medical alarm and protection company. The commercial showed an elderly woman falling to the floor, unable to get up. With no other recourse, she activates the pendant around her neck provided by the company to connect her with an emergency dispatcher, who promptly sends help to rescue her.

Unlike the scenario in the commercial, we don't have a button to push that will summon help when we've been emotionally and mentally defeated. All we have is our own willpower.

~ Life had weakened me and forced me to my knees. The energy to fight had departed me as I found myself drowning in the sea of anger and overcome by the thrashing waves of disappointment, sadness, and vengeful thoughts. Facing the loss of my home and my marriage, I blamed everyone else for my current and past mishaps.

I faulted my stepfather for failing to be an adequate father-figure. His wrongdoings predestined a bleak existence that I had attempted to escape many times. If I hadn't undergone his malicious actions and psychologically debilitating words, I may have lived a normal life. Perhaps then, I would have known about love, and in turn, my wife and I would have lived peacefully and happily. Instead, I only knew how to express my love through sex, manipulation, deception, and verbal assaults, as with all my other past relationships.

I blamed my mother for terminating her parental rights. A more courageous act, such as ridding her life of my stepfather, Cheetah, would have spared me from assuming the responsibility of providing for my siblings at the age of 13. An honorable yet sacrificial action prevented me from experiencing a fun, mischievous adolescence as my friends had.

I also blamed the Department of Social Health Services and the Child Protection Services. If these entities had helped me establish a stable life after aging out of the foster care system, I wouldn't have experienced homelessness. I wouldn't have had to live penniless and wondered where my next meal would come from. Perhaps then I could have jump-started my life and fulfilled my vision of going to college after high school.

I even condemned my ex-wife for her cowardice. Moving out of the house without respectfully saying goodbye drained me emotionally. Whatever happened to "til death do us part?"

Last, I blamed God, the all-loving, all-knowing, and all-powerful, omnipotent Being, for giving me an unfavorable hand and taking away the people whom I trusted, loved, and felt secure. If he hadn't taken my great grandparents, Pappa and Mother, away from me, I might have had a blissful youth. I wished that I could've had a real shot at a happier life.

The weight of misery can keep us from lifting our heads up high enough to see the signs of hope. Many of us have fallen emotionally, mentally, and financially, and we have stayed down for so long that we found comfort on the cold floor of anguish. *When will we take responsibility for our lives?* We must not blame other people or our past circumstances for our current predicaments; rather, we should focus on getting back up again.

How to Get Back Up Again

"If you get up one more time than you fall you will make it through."

-Chinese Proverb

Life is filled with robbers and thieves wearing the clothes of unfortunate circumstances and adversity to knock us down as they steal our happiness. In exchange for our joy, they leave us misery, smiles for tears, and financial stability for economic destitution.

Eventually, we'll encounter and be knocked down by one or more of these culprits. When we do fall, it's our responsibility to rise again. Some of us might feel that our own flaws or the faults of others make getting back up an insurmountable task. We allow painful heartaches, failed business ventures, and other adversities to paralyze us, instilling fear and a sense of helplessness. However, it's only our decision to remain down that can truly keep us there. One of the most effective ways to get back up again is to nurture our spiritual growth.

Growing Spiritually

"What lies behind us and what lies before us are tiny matters compared with what lies within us."

-Oliver Wendell Holmes

Spiritual growth is essential in helping us get back up again. The condition of your spirit will determine whether you can or cannot overcome and combat adversity or affliction.

~ As a foster child, my foster parents took me to church every Sunday. Why? I have no idea. When I asked my foster mother the purpose behind going to church so often, she said, "Because you need God in your life!

Little to her knowledge, I detested God for His failure to stop the chaos from happening in my young life. Called a Heavenly Father and Protector by the church community, God hadn't protected my family from anything. He let my stepfather molest my 11-year-old sister repeatedly. He permitted my stepfather to beat my mother without remorse. He allowed a grown man to molest me. He gave my mother the okay to terminate her parental rights, which led to my (and my siblings') coerced stay in a broken system. Having God in my life when I thought He was, did not make me anxious to go to church.

Consequently, years later into my adult life, the breakdown of my marriage forced me to reconsider accepting God. If He really existed, I needed Him to help me. I had grown tired of living with the hurt and pain associated with my past. I no longer wanted to hurt the people I loved. Moreover, I wanted to be rid of the self-loathing that drove me to many self-destructive activities. I tried counseling, but it only confirmed how messed up and broken I really was. I had nowhere else to turn.

As I sat on the living room floor, crying uncontrollably, I remembered the words of my late foster mother: "You need God in your life!" Then, something weird happened. A small voice within me said, "Get up and take a walk!" Startled by the command, I dried my eyes and left home.

I walked to the corner of the block and then headed up the little hill. A building on my left, from which the sounds of drums and singing escaped through the door, caught my attention. The larger of the two signs read, "Lost Sheep Ministries," and the other, "You have just taken your first step in faith!"

Grudgingly, I entered and took a seat nearest to the door. Eyes closed, I listened to the music as I cried. I had never felt so grieved. Following the choir's musical selection, Pastor Gary Hay, Sr. approached the podium. He opened, "Regardless of what you are going through, God is still on the throne. When you can't control the things that are facing you, give them to God…"

Following the end of the service, I spoke with the pastor and asked him if he could teach me how to grow spiritually. He looked at me compassionately as if the sorrow on my face told him everything I had going on inside of me. "It's not an overnight process," he said. "But if you keep coming, God will give you the breakthrough you're after."

Pastor Hay mentored me for seven years. The initial years were tough. I had to confront all my mistakes and past struggles and really examine myself. He pushed me to shift my perspective on my past and present situations. I had to focus on compassion instead of seeking revenge. I had to practice love without expecting anything in return. Most importantly, I had to believe in my capacity for improvement—to seek constructive solutions rather than resorting to destructive actions. The adage, "You can't teach old dogs new tricks," is partly true. If the old dog is willing to learn, he'll become receptive to new teachings.

It's Not about Religion

"True religion is real living; living with all one's soul, with all one's goodness and righteousness."

-Albert Einstein

Using spiritual growth as a tool for *getting back up* might seem to carry religious connotations, but it doesn't necessarily do so. We all have diverse thoughts and beliefs about religion. However, the focus here isn't about embracing or dismissing any religious teachings; it's about recognizing the healing and life-improving benefits that spiritual growth can bring. These transformative effects are attained by engaging in two crucial tasks: renewing our minds and applying the wisdom gained from overcoming hardships.

Renewing Our Minds: The First Step of Growing Spiritually

"Do not be conformed to this world, but be transformed by the renewal of your mind, that by testing you may discern what is the will of God, what is good and acceptable and perfect."

-Romans 12:2 ESV

Contrary to common belief, our thoughts manifest into physical actions. For instance, if we convince ourselves that we're unworthy of a great partner or career opportunity, our behavior will reflect that belief. We might seem closed off, communicate with uncertainty, or gravitate toward unhealthy relationships. Despite having the potential to attain anything we desire, our negative thought patterns can prevent us from reaching our goals. Consider Jenny's situation:

~ When I first laid eyes on Calvin, it felt like my heart skipped a beat. His confident and dreamy brown eyes were both captivating and inviting. My girlfriends thought I had met my perfect match, and I couldn't help but agree. Calvin, a high-level executive at a marketing firm, exuded charm and sophistication with his sharp attire. He was utterly irresistible, so when he asked me out, I couldn't say no.

About a year into dating Calvin, I discovered I was eight weeks pregnant. I believed this news would strengthen our bond, but I was mistaken. What followed was beyond anything I could have anticipated.

I invited Calvin over for dinner with the intention of sharing the good news. After we finished dessert, we moved to the couch. Excitedly, I told him, "I have something to show you."

"What is it, hon?" he replied and smiled.

I quickly went to the bathroom and returned with the home pregnancy test results. "I'm pregnant!" I exclaimed, showing him the two blue lines.

Since Calvin had always expressed a desire for children, I expected him to share in the joy of the news. He didn't. Instead, he looked at me with a strange expression, rose abruptly, and walked over to the fireplace.

"What's wrong?" I asked, trying to bring his attention back to me. "I thought you'd be happy!"

Calvin stayed silent, avoiding eye contact. When I touched his shoulder, his reaction shocked me.

"Get your hands off me!" he yelled, abruptly turning toward me. "What? You think this is some kind of game? Are you trying to trap me?"

Naturally, I was taken aback, completely surprised by his reaction.

"I won't tolerate being spoken to like that, Calvin! What's the issue? You've always talked about wanting children, about being a father, and now you have the opportunity!"

"You need to get an abortion!" he hollered.

"No! What's wrong with you?"

"No?" Calvin mocked me as he slowly approached.

"No! I will not!"

I couldn't believe what unfolded next. The man I loved, the one I envisioned sharing my life with, struck me across the face, shoved me to the ground, and viciously kicked me in the stomach. In desperation, I grabbed his foot and caused him to stumble. But as I tried to flee, he pulled me back, continuing to assault me with slaps and punches.

His abuse led to the loss of the baby and caused internal hemorrhaging, putting my life in jeopardy. Despite knowing I should have left Calvin for his behavior, I didn't. Instead, I blamed myself for that night and took full responsibility for his actions.

It took me three years to gather the courage to call the police on Calvin. By then, I had endured 28 beatings during our relationship. Some of the abuse left me with a dislocated jaw, two broken ribs, and a concussion. When it was all over, my friends couldn't believe what had happened and asked why I stayed. "I loved him," I replied, "and maybe I deserved it. I thought it was the price I had to pay to be with such a great man." Looking back, I realize how flawed my thinking was.

Tears streamed down my face as I listened to Jenny recount her experiences of abuse. Her words brought back vivid memories of every punch, kick, and slap my stepfather inflicted on my mother.

When we lack positive self-perception and fail to envision our desires, we invite misfortune and undesired situations into our lives. However, when we recognize our worth, as Jenny eventually did, we start to attract the kind of lives we desire. At the writing, Jenny has married the true love of her life, is a proud mother of two girls, and helps abused women with restoring joy to their lives.

Knowing Your Value

"The words 'I am' are potent words; be careful what you hitch them to. The thing you're claiming has a way of reaching back and claiming you."

-A. L. Kitselman

To renew our minds, we need to focus on understanding our own values. The value we place on ourselves communicates to the world the kind of people and opportunities we're willing to accept. Unfortunately, many of us undervalue ourselves, settling for less than what we deserve in terms of happiness, and as a result, we become susceptible to anguish and sadness.

~ I finally snapped out of my defeatist mindset. For so long, I believed I wasn't worthy of a fulfilling life. But then I realized that my worth isn't defined by past relationships or financial struggles—it's up to me to determine. With this revelation, I began to see myself in a new light. I deserved a loving partner. I deserved financial independence. I had the potential to become a great leader, speaker, and writer. After this transformative realization, I turned to one of the most impactful quotes I've ever read by Marianne Williamson:

"Our deepest fear is not that we are inadequate. Our deepest fear is that we are powerful beyond measure. It is our light, not

our darkness that frightens us most. We ask ourselves, 'Who am I to be brilliant, gorgeous, talented, and famous?' Actually, who are you not to be? You are a child of God. Your playing small does not serve the world. There is nothing enlightened about shrinking so that people won't feel insecure around you. We were born to make manifest the glory of God that is within us. It's not just in some of us; it's in all of us. And when we let our own light shine, we unconsciously give other people permission to do the same. As we are liberated from our own fear, our presence automatically liberates others."

I keep this quote visible and read it frequently, especially when negative thoughts of discouragement, inadequacy, discontent, and unhappiness arise. It helps me remember my true identity, what I deserve, and why I need to continue pushing forward. As a result, my negative thoughts don't linger for long.

If you were to liken yourself to highly prized, high-quality jewelry, what would you be? Some may see themselves as diamonds, others as gold, and some as platinum. Just as these precious jewels demand special care and attention, shouldn't we also expect life to treat us as rare gems? Unfortunately, it can't do so unless we first recognize our own value. What is your worth?

Apply the Wisdom of Suffering: The Second Step of Growing Spiritually

"By three methods we may learn wisdom: first, by reflection, which is noblest; second, by imitation, which is easiest; and third, by experience, which is the most bitter."

-Confucius

In the world of spiritual development, pain and suffering teach us wisdom— "the accumulated knowledge or erudition or enlightenment"—which is an essential ingredient in restoring our lives. For example, painful experiences help us recognize our inner imbalances, guide us to redefine our perceptions of "what's most important," and urge us to rediscover the invaluable qualities we have to offer ourselves and the world.

However, the application of wisdom from suffering comes with its own set of challenges. Many of us who suffer from afflictions and adversity turn to our own methods of numbing ourselves rather than ask the question, "How can I use this pain to further impact the quality of my life positively?" My lovely wife, Kim, often poses this question to herself.

~ 6, 4, 7, 10, 16, 21, 24, 31...

My life has felt like a string of lottery numbers, each representing the age at which I was told my life would end. From four months old to my current age of 45, I've received predictions of my demise.

At just four months old, I was diagnosed with sickle-cell anemia. I had to endure hearing doctors deliver discouraging statements to me and my parents, like "She won't survive,"

"We've exhausted all options," and "I'm sorry, there's nothing more we can do."

During severe painful episodes known as "crises," when Sickle Cell takes over my body, causing hospitalization for days or even weeks, I pray for peace in both my body and spirit. At times, I've felt like I was facing death. However, I decided long ago that I have a purpose to fulfill in this life, and I refuse to let my illness defeat me. Therefore, I've taken it upon myself to empower others with this disease by advocating for various organizations dedicated to finding a cure. Despite what doctors may say, I am not succumbing to Sickle Cell; I am living with it, and I refuse to be a victim—I will continue to prevail for my child, my husband, and those in the sickle cell community!

The concept of "wisdom from suffering" suggests that we should change our attitudes toward our circumstances. It teaches us that we're being prepared for a higher purpose and encourages us to seek ways to heal ourselves by assisting others in their struggles. This wisdom emphasizes the significance of nurturing qualities like optimism, hope, faith, resilience, and vision. As mentioned in Galatians 5:22-23, attributes associated with wisdom include "love, joy, peace, patience, kindness, goodness, faithfulness, gentleness, and self-control."

Take heart in knowing that your suffering is not permanent; it will ultimately guide you toward a more fulfilling life and lead you to fulfill your destiny.

Yes, We Can!

"Our own thoughts of being great are the only voices we should listen to!"

-LaDon

Regardless of your political beliefs, there's much to learn from the powerful and emotionally charged speech delivered by former President Barack Obama before his 2008 presidency win. The essence of his message was that despite our hardships, we have the power to change our trajectory in life. We can pivot our lives starting from the moment we choose to emerge from the darkness of uncertainty, hopelessness, and discouragement, becoming our own champions of success.

"...but in the unlikely story that is America, there has never been anything false about hope. For when we have faced down impossible odds; when we've been told that we're not ready, or that we shouldn't try, or that we can't, generations of Americans have responded with a simple creed that sums up the spirit of a people...Yes We Can!"

No matter the sleepless nights, the anxiety about tomorrow, or the seemingly insurmountable challenges ahead, we can rebuild our lives if we simply rise again. It takes time to renew our minds and apply the wisdom gained from suffering, as we must recondition ourselves to respond differently during times of hardship. Despite the difficulty, it is achievable. There's nothing beyond the capability of the human spirit. Let's quiet the thoughts that hinder our progress by affirming, "Yes, I can!"

Chapter 8
Evolve into Your True Self

"So God created man in his own image, in the image of God he created him; male and female..."

-Genesis 1:27

The quote beneath the heading of this chapter holds more significance than you realize, as it unveils the genuine truth about our identity.

When we contemplate the concept of God's image, many of us (who believe in the divine) would describe it as powerful, loving, incredible, comforting, and enlightening. Consider this: you were formed in this very image. This doesn't mean you're a deity, but rather, you possess the inherent ability to shape the life you desire, regardless of your circumstances. Despite being created in this powerful image, many of us struggle to grasp this truth due to identity issues. We wrestle between *"Who we think we are"* and *"Who we truly are."*

Who We Think We Are

"They say I am, therefore, I must be!"

-Ginelle Wymin

Who we think we are conflicts with *who we really are*. Many of us harbor inaccurate self-images and flawed perceptions of ourselves, as discussed in Chapter Six, "Reject Doubt," due to the influence of our environments. These surroundings can limit our ability to fully realize our true selves. Consequently, we may find ourselves content in unhealthy situations, engaging in socially inappropriate behavior, or settling for lifestyles that fall short of what we truly deserve.

~ Not long ago, I agreed to speak at a graduation ceremony for men who were formerly incarcerated and transitioning back into society. As I got out of my car, I crossed the street toward The House where the ceremony was being held. A thin young man came up to me.

"Are you from the airline company?" he asked, eyeing my suit.

"No," I said with a smile, "I'm here for the party."

"Oh," he replied, as if surprised. "I didn't think you would come. Everyone else who was supposed to speak today canceled on us. I don't blame them. Who would want to be in a room full of criminals? You can turn back, too, if you'd like. I won't tell anyone you were here."

"My man," I chuckled. "It'll take more than your friends to stop me from attending this ceremony."

"So, you're not afraid?" he asked, looking directly into my eyes.

"If you knew my family and where I come from," I laughed, "I'd ask you the same."

He shook his head, smiling.

"Follow me," he gestured. "I'll show you where we're going!"

The young man led me to the program director. After exchanging greetings, he pulled me aside.

"These men are eager to hear what you have to say," he explained. "They've been disappointed by several other cancellations, so their morale is a bit low."

"Let's do something about that," I said with a smile.

The program director ushered me into a room where most of the men were enjoying chicken and watching a movie. After they finished eating, he switched off the television and addressed them. "Gentlemen," he began, as I stood near the window with my hands clasped behind my back, "I have a special guest today... I present to you, Mr. Ellard Thomas!"

After shaking hands with the program director, I faced the eager crowd.

"Who am I standing in front of?" I inquired.

The room fell silent.

"What do you mean?" one gentleman in the far back asked.

"Criminals," an older man shouted. "You're standing in front of criminals!"

The men grumbled; some nodded in agreement.

"Why would you say that?" I asked.

"Besides the stupid shit we got caught for," he said, folding his arms, "that's what society says we are. No matter what we do, we'll always be criminals!"

"But are you truly a criminal?" I asked the group; each man fell silent.

I glanced around the room. Each man stared back, patiently awaiting my response. I reflected on the information the program director had shared with me about the attendees.

"I don't see a room filled with criminals," I exclaimed. "I see a room filled with fathers, aspiring entrepreneurs, and men striving to rebuild their lives. I see men who were once held back from achieving greatness because they made decisions based on who they thought they were, not who they truly are..."

The men leaned in; some started jotting down notes. A glimmer of hope reignited their aspirations.

"Just because you made a mistake," I reengaged, "you don't have to be defined by it. Within you is an incredible individual who's been waiting for this moment for a long time—a second chance to do something phenomenal..."

Following the one-hour speech-turned-workshop, each man realized what he needed to do to begin living out who he truly was.

"Mr. Thomas," an attendee hollered with a deep voice, approaching me slowly.

"Yes," I responded, watching him make his way toward me.

My eyes followed the massive-sized, dark-skinned man until he stood before me.

"Sir, I have been around for a very long time," he stated, "and I have never met anyone like you. I've been hurt by a lot of people, and I have hurt a lot of people in my past. I served 15 years for some dumb shit I had no business doing. I won't go into that, but I needed to look you in your eyes to see if you're real!"

"What do you see?" I asked, meeting his unwavering stare.

"A real muthafucka," he responded.

I extended my hand and was ill-prepared for what was to come. The burly gentleman grabbed me and hugged me tightly.

"Thank you for today," he cried, loosening his grip. "Thank you.

Once I finished shaking hands and speaking with the rest of the group, I watched each man mingle with family, children, significant others, and friends. It was truly a remarkable sight— one many people would never see.

Our self-perceptions can be shaped by our past experiences, societal influences, or challenging circumstances. However, we don't have to simply accept these perceptions as our true selves. For instance, the gentleman who believed I was addressing a room full of criminals had accepted the idea of being a criminal himself. He didn't realize that he held a false image of who he was, much like one of his fellow attendees, Ron.

~ As a child, Ron had dreams of becoming a mechanic like his father. He loved the idea of building and fixing cars with his hands.

Unfortunately, when cars became more mechanically sophisticated, there was no place in the market for Ron's uneducated father. As a result, he was fired. Rather than finding the resources to help him familiarize himself with the new technological advances, Ron's dad turned to the occupation of robbing and stealing as a means of earning money. Inevitably, the police apprehended him following a strong-arm robbery, which resulted in Ron's father serving 20 years in prison.

Often told by his mother that he would end up just like his father, Ron abandoned the idea of being a mechanic. He thought this type of work would push him into a life of crime. Therefore, he skipped the idea of pursuing his passion and jumped into the criminal world. Starting out stealing mail from neighbors' mailboxes, Ron graduated to pickpocketing, carjacking, and later burglary. Just like his father, he ended up in jail.

When we succumb to and accept the perceptions of outside influences as our own, we become thrown into a world of confusion. We then live our lives based on others' definitions and opinions of who we are. As a result, we sabotage any chance at living the lives we desire.

Become Who You Truly Are

"Never be bullied into silence. Never allow yourself to be made a victim. Accept no one's definition of your life; define yourself."

-*Harvey Fierstein*

Each of us has experienced or are currently facing hardships. Unfortunately, these hardships have shaped the way we think and behave and have hindered us from getting closer to our true selves. We are not truly abusive, irrational, inadequate, violent, uncaring, or incapable people. Many of us have been misled to believe we're something we're not and have accepted these imposed beliefs as truths. That said, we must decide to transform into our true selves just as Pyllo, the caterpillar, does.

~ For most of his life, Pyllo, the caterpillar, is an unattractive creature, creeping along the ground and passively accepting whatever fate brings his way. Predators see him as an easy meal due to his slow movements and lack of defense mechanisms. Opportunities for growth and change seem scarce for this small creature.

Having narrowly escaped becoming a meal for predators, Pyllo eventually enters a cocoon—the pupal stage, serving as the transformative bridge between his current form and his true essence.

During this stage, he undergoes a remarkable metamorphosis from a humble creature to a stunningly beautiful addition to the wonders of nature. Emerging as a butterfly, his true self, Pyllo gains the freedom to soar and explore at will, shedding the shell that symbolizes his past struggles with fear and uncertainty.

Many of us resemble Pyllo in some ways. In our current false identities, we struggle with indecision and lack success due to our fears and apprehensions. Just like Pyllo's limited agility as a caterpillar left him vulnerable to predators, we'll also find ourselves unable to escape the threats of failure, defeat, falsehoods, and discontentment. Until we go through our own transformative journey, where we undergo shaping and change, we'll remain as we are, only dreaming of living a different life.

The Cocoon—The Realization of Who We Truly Are

"First comes thought; then organization of that thought, into ideas and plans; then transformation of those plans into reality. The beginning, as you will observe, is in your imagination."

-Napoleon Hill

Like Pyllo's cocoon, which served as a protective shell for his transformation, our cocoon represents the moment we realize our true selves. It's when we become fully conscious of our inner greatness and potential. The reflection of the mirror no longer reveals a false image but presents an individual of great worth, whether a business professional, loving spouse, compassionate parent, wise mentor, or incredible contributor to society. While in this state of mind, we see ourselves as successful, happy, enlightened, and strong. We become hopeful of things to come. We become receptive to and welcome the possibility of personal and professional restoration. As a result, we dissolve our self-sabotaging beliefs and begin changing how we perceive ourselves and our conditions.

~ Enduring years of physical and sexual abuse didn't lead me to a life of crime. Crippling heartaches from failed relationships and the collapse of my marriage didn't stop me from desiring love again. Multiple job losses and failed business opportunities didn't prevent me from investing again. Losing loved ones who truly cared about me didn't halt my desire to live life. Discouraging words from those who doubted my ability to become a writer or speaker, although upsetting, didn't keep me from writing this book.

Had I not come to realize who I truly am, I might have taken a different path. The person I once believed myself to be was already on the road to self-destruction, but fortunately, I underwent a transformation into my authentic self.

Regardless of where you currently stand—whether it's in your personal, professional, spiritual, or financial life—it's crucial to recognize your inherent value. The person you were in the past doesn't define the greatness of who you truly are. Don't allow anyone or anything to diminish or obscure this truth.

Evolution—The Manifestation of the Inevitable

"All my life I had been looking for something, and everywhere I turned, someone tried to tell me what it was. I accepted their answers too, though they were often in contradiction and even self-contradictory. I was naïve. I was looking for myself and asking everyone except myself questions which I, and only I, could answer. It took me a long time and much painful boomeranging of my expectations to achieve a realization everyone else appears to have been born with: that I am nobody, but myself."

-Ralph Ellison, "Battle Royal"

I remember a conversation I had with my former mother-in-law. It's interesting how a few words exchanged in that conversation would later profoundly affect my life.

~ I had come over to visit Ma Dukes (a name I had given her) as my wife went to get her hair and nails done.

"Ma Dukes?" I said as she prepared dinner.

"Yes, son," she answered.

"I believe I have completed everything I was designed for."

Ma Dukes smiled, turning her attention to her meal.

"Ellard," she said softly, "you haven't arrived yet!"

"What do you mean?" I asked.

"You're still young. Despite all you have undergone and accomplished, you haven't become the man God has designed you to be. The greatness within you has not surfaced, but it will eventually!"

I shrugged my shoulders and shifted the conversation to another topic. At the time, her words didn't make much sense to me, but it wasn't until years later that their significance became clear.

Ma Dukes, with her deep wisdom, must have sensed the profound challenges that would shape me into the man I am today—a person driven by purpose, vision, encouragement, compassion, sensitivity, integrity, and confidence. It's possible she also perceived that I was merely going through the motions of existence rather than truly living. I wish she could have warned me about what was to come: my brief marriage to her daughter.

Once we begin living authentically as our true selves, the journey doesn't end there. We must consistently maintain our greatness, as life will continually challenge the integrity of our newfound perspectives.

To transition into and maintain our true selves effectively, we should consistently apply the six principles of courage outlined earlier. These principles serve as guiding lights, helping us navigate the complexities of life with authenticity and resilience. By embracing courage in our actions, thoughts, and decisions, we steadily align ourselves with our genuine identity, fostering growth, fulfillment, and lasting transformation.

Choose: The First Principle of Courage

The ability to choose grants us the opportunity to start afresh and confront our fears about the future. These choices lay the groundwork for rebuilding our lives. While some decisions may seem daunting and distressing, resigning ourselves to unhappiness and undesirable circumstances is not an option. It's important to embrace the power of choice and take decisive steps toward a brighter, more fulfilling future.

If we hesitate to make the necessary choices to achieve our goals, we have no one to blame but ourselves. It's our responsibility to decide whether the effort required to become our authentic selves is worthwhile. Often, our reluctance to evolve stems from laziness or a fear of acknowledging and addressing our challenges.

Oppose Failure: The Second Principle of Courage

Every decision we make opens the door to potential failure. Challenges and setbacks are part of life's journey and cannot be avoided. However, we should not allow these obstacles to become excuses for cowardice. Instead, we must confront difficult circumstances with a steadfast resolve to pursue our happiness. With determination, we can overcome life's attempts to obstruct our success. Let's refuse to let hardships triumph over us and become a formidable force against adversity.

Use the Power of Negative Emotions for Positive Action: The Third Principle of Courage

Each setback we face has the potential to evoke strong negative emotions within us. These emotions can sometimes lead us to engage in self-destructive behaviors like excessive

ELLARD "COACH ELL" THOMAS

smoking, unhealthy eating, substance abuse, or violence. As emotional beings, it's natural to feel disappointment, anger, betrayal, or dissatisfaction. However, instead of succumbing to these emotions, we can harness their power to propel us toward our goals. One way to do this is by referring to your *alternative actions list.*

Reject Doubt: The Fourth Principle of Courage

Regardless of how many times we may fail to achieve a certain desire or how difficult our past experiences have been, we can still create the lives we truly desire. Instead of being consumed by doubt, we can tap into our inherent power and live out our destinies. The key to achieving this lies in rejecting doubt and embracing belief. By acknowledging and dispelling our self-limiting beliefs and adopting a new narrative, we can align ourselves with our visions for the future. Remember, belief is the fundamental ingredient in overcoming doubt.

Acknowledge Your Strong Whys: The Fifth Principle of Courage

Amidst the weight of negativity, fatigue, and daunting circumstances, it's crucial to keep in mind the reasons, individuals, and goals that drive us to restore and reconstruct our lives. These sources of inspiration are like vital sustenance; they provide the strength we need to overcome the challenges we inevitably face.

Our *strong whys* are as essential as the air we breathe. When we feel depleted and unable to continue, these external wellsprings of strength reignite our resolve and counteract thoughts of giving up. They propel us forward, even when all signs suggest we should halt. By staying connected to our reasons for overcoming adversity and pursuing happiness, nothing can hinder our progress.

Get Back Up Again: The Sixth Principle of Courage

Rarely do we achieve our desired outcomes on the first try. Sometimes, reaching the lives we desire demands a second, third, fourth, or even fiftieth attempt. Many failed endeavors in love, finances, and other aspects of happiness may cause us to stumble. However, the key is to get back up again.

Getting back up again requires spiritual growth, which involves freeing our minds from limiting beliefs and embracing the wisdom gained from adversity. Here, suffering encompasses any undesirable emotion or circumstance that hinders our happiness. Through spiritual growth, your inner resilience is fortified, empowering you to enhance the quality of your life.

Evolve into Your True Self: The Seventh Principle of Courage

Despite the negative self-perceptions that often cloud our minds, we possess immense power to manifest our thoughts into reality. The discrepancy between who we believe ourselves to be and who we truly are is a common struggle. Despite our past experiences or present situations, we are not unlovable, broken, unattractive, destitute, unworthy, or incapable. We are incredible, phenomenal, wonderful, intelligent, inquisitive and excellent.

Allowing external influences and others' judgments to define us has obscured our perception of the greatness that resides within us.

Despite the challenges we've faced in our lives, we belong to an exceptional group of individuals who, through steadfast adherence to the other six principles, embody qualities such as love, capability, leadership, worthiness, attractiveness, affection, ambition, success, happiness, power, courage, peace, faith, opportunism, imagination, and creativity. Embracing our true selves allows us to see opportunities where others might only see setbacks or misfortune.

Whenever you encounter hardships or obstacles, remind yourself of your true identity. An individual who knows their worth and true essence cannot be defeated by adversity.

The Road Less Traveled

*"Let your mind start a journey through a strange new world.
Leave all thoughts of the world you knew before. Let your soul
take you where you long to be...Close your eyes, let your spirit
start to soar, and you'll live as you've never lived before."*

-Erich Fromm

Even with guidance or a roadmap to lead us toward our true selves, many of us falter on the journey. We may find the process daunting, too painful, or too demanding, convincing ourselves that settling for less is acceptable. However, such resignation ultimately leads to a life marred by regret.

Becoming our true and authentic selves demands a willingness to embrace tasks that others shy away from. We must make tough decisions, confront failure head-on, and harness our negative emotions for growth rather than destruction. Rejecting doubt and arming ourselves with our strongest motivations are essential steps on this path.

Moreover, persistence is key. We must be prepared to rise time and again, undeterred by setbacks, until we achieve our desired outcomes. In life, quitting is the only endeavor that requires no effort, while true transformation demands resilience and unwavering determination. Robert Frost's poem, *The Road Not Taken,* illustrates this point.

> Two roads diverged in a yellow wood,
> And sorry I could not travel both
> And be one traveler, long I stood
> And looked down one as far as I could
> To where it bent in the undergrowth;
>
> Then took the other, as just as fair,
> And having perhaps the better claim
> Because it was grassy and wanted wear,
> Though as for that the passing there
> Had worn them really about the same,
>
> And both that morning equally lay
> In leaves no step had trodden black.
> Oh, I marked the first for another day!
> Yet knowing how way leads on to way
> I doubted if I should ever come back.
>
> I shall be telling this with a sigh

Somewhere ages and ages hence:
Two roads diverged in a wood, and I,
I took the one less traveled by,
And that has made all the difference.

You are currently standing at a pivotal moment in your life, faced with a crucial decision. You can either accept your present circumstances as an unchangeable fate or choose to embark on a transformative journey toward realizing your true potential. However, transitioning from who you are now to the empowered individual you're meant to be is no simple feat. It demands courage, resilience, and a willingness to confront the unknown.

Despite the challenges that lie ahead, the journey promises invaluable rewards. By bravely tackling obstacles and refusing to yield to doubt or fear, you can gradually unveil your authentic self and manifest your deepest aspirations. Though the road may be difficult, each step forward brings you closer to the realization of your dreams.

Let us embrace this journey wholeheartedly, knowing that the destination holds immeasurable promise. Together, let us rise above adversity and emerge as the empowered individuals we are destined to become.

Chapter 9
Mastering the Art of Living Courageously

"My life is my message!"

-Gandhi

Life is fleeting, and every moment counts. We simply cannot afford to dwell in negativity, anger, or any other state that opposes happiness. Nor can we squander our valuable time assigning blame to others for our own unproductive or self-destructive actions. It's important that we seize each moment to cultivate positivity, contentment, and constructive behaviors, thereby embracing the full richness of life. We must keep **moving forward courageously**.

Throughout this book, we've delved into the fundamental principles essential for reclaiming and revitalizing our lives. Some of these principles may have sparked introspection, while others may have stirred feelings of unease. Nevertheless, the purpose of these principles is to empower you to pursue your aspirations even amidst adversity and hardship.

As emphasized earlier in this book, living a fulfilling life after facing adversity requires courage. Although we may wish for a life free from complications, such a notion is unrealistic; denying this reality is merely self-deception.

Living courageously, as we'll explore, is a skill that must be honed. Mastering this skill entails consistently applying the seven principles of courageous advancement. There's no "one-time use and done" solution because life presents myriad challenges that can threaten our happiness. Therefore, we must equip ourselves with these "secrets," internalizing them, keeping them close, and practicing them daily to navigate life's twists and turns with resilience and fortitude.

Stating the Obvious

"Ninety percent of the world's woe comes from people not knowing themselves, their abilities, their frailties, and even their real virtues. Most of us go almost all the way through life as complete strangers to ourselves -- so how can we know anyone else?"

-Sidney J. Harris

The seven principles of advancing courageously aren't groundbreaking concepts; rather, we've likely utilized some of these methods in our past experiences. Reflecting on moments of triumph over adversity, we can readily identify the first principle: choice. The subsequent principles serve as a roadmap for navigating future challenges we'll undoubtedly encounter. Genuine self-improvement occurs when we acknowledge that the key to success, love, and happiness lies within us, not solely in external sources like books. Books should serve as reminders of this truth, reinforcing the importance of principles such as those encapsulated in the seven principles of courage.

Living is a Gift

"You don't get to choose how you're going to die, or when. You can only decide how you're going to live. Now."

-Joan Baez

Living may not always feel like a gift, but it truly is. Each day presents us with the chance to refine our identities and uncover what brings us joy. Every challenge we face serves as a lesson in love, happiness, purpose, and impacting others. Despite feeling like life has dealt us an unfair hand at times, does this diminish the fact that our lives, despite hardships, are gifts?

As we contemplate our fresh outlooks on life, let's take a break from dwelling on our difficulties and recognize the abundance of gifts surrounding us: the air we breathe, the presence of loved ones, the chance to grow spiritually, the support of friends and family, the lessons learned from past setbacks, the power of imagination, and everything else that contributes to our personal growth and success. Even during moments when life feels challenging, we are still granted the opportunity to enhance our lives for the better.

Keep Moving Forward, Courageously

"The action required to sustain human life is primarily intellectual,everything man needs has to be discovered by his mind and produced by his effort."

-Ayn Rand

As our journey together ends, I feel compelled to share a poignant memory from my mentorship with Coach, my business mentor. This recollection serves as a constant reminder of the importance of courage and resilience in my daily life. It encapsulates the transformative power of the seven principles of courage and the profound impact they have had on my journey toward my true self.

~ As I sit at my desk, eagerly awaiting Coach's arrival, impatience creeps in. Glancing out of the window, I observe a sudden downpour engulfing the city. Cars on the road hastily flick on their hazard lights to navigate the slippery conditions and avoid potential accidents.

As I observe light poles and street signs swaying in the heavy gusts, a sense of urgency grips me. I dash to the rear of the building, hoping to find Coach in his office. Disappointingly, his office is empty. I try calling him on his cell phone, but there's no answer.

Curious if Coach is outside, I open the door and witness a remarkable scene. With one hand clutching his bowler hat to prevent it from being whisked away by the wind and the other gripping his cane for support, Coach leans into the fierce winds. Despite momentarily being pushed back, he persists, gradually regaining his footing and forging ahead.

I rush to assist Coach, nearly crashing into the drenched, elderly figure. Offering my arm, I shout, "Take my arm!" He pays no heed to my gesture and presses on. Determined, I accompany him, braving the powerful gusts together.

Amidst the chaos of flying tree branches and swaying power lines, Coach turns to me with a smile.

"It's all part of life," he yells over the roaring wind, retrieving his fallen sign. "The sun will return, Ellard. We just gotta keep moving forward, courageously, until it does."

I pause, briefly puzzled by his statement, but soon find his words resonating with me.

The Sun Will Return

"There has to be evil so that good can prove its purity above it."

-Buddha

Nothing lasts forever. Even the most destructive storms eventually pass. However, amid our pain and suffering, it's easy to lose sight of this truth and become consumed by the havoc the storms wreak.

~ When my ex-wife ended our marriage, I experienced an emotional pain unlike anything I had felt before. Days passed without eating or sleeping, and each moment felt like an eternity of agony.

In the weeks after the divorce, my family started expressing concern for my well-being. I had shed 20 pounds, hoping that somehow the pain would lessen. It didn't.

However, one day, I had a breakthrough. With the support of my close friends and family, I came to realize that I was a good person, regardless of the difficulties I faced in my marriage. I had endured prolonged suffering because I carried the weight of both my wife's and my own marital mistakes. Years later, I find myself healthier and happier than I ever imagined possible, and I am committed to maintaining this state. I have found happiness once more in marriage, now with a beautiful and loving wife by my side. Additionally, I am blessed to be the proud father of a handsome son.

The storm I faced eventually passed, and I believe yours will too. It's important to keep reminding yourself that you have the strength to overcome it!

In the face of adversity's strong winds and rains, it's easy to feel pushed back or knocked down, as if our suffering has no end. But before you surrender to despair, hold on to the certainty that the sun will return. Until it does, press onward with courage. As we bid farewell, here's an inspirational quote to keep in mind:

"The seeds of greatness are often watered by the rains of adversity. From these treacherous conditions, in which hope seems to run down the sewer drains of life, will emerge kingly men and queenly women, once unknown to themselves and others, who will remind the world of the endless possibilities hidden within misfortune. May their enchanting voices of victory echo throughout the generations to come—to tell them that the power to walk and dance on the clouds of happiness resides within their minds, spirits, and souls—not on the rocky cliffs of other people's thoughts and abilities!"

-Ellard "Coach Ell" Thomas

Special Prayer for You

"Prayer is more than meditation. In meditation, the source of strength is one's self. When one prays, he goes to a source of strength greater than his own."

-Madame de Stael

As mentioned earlier in this book, prayer has been a cornerstone of my life. I've experienced firsthand its ability to bring healing, success, favor, wisdom, and happiness. Regardless of your personal faith or beliefs, I believe it's important to offer prayers for your current healing and restoration, as well as for your future success and happiness. Please take a moment to read the prayer dedicated to you, and may you find the strength of belief to see it come to fruition.

(Prayer for him)

Heavenly Father,

I come before you to pray for the blessings upon this remarkable man. Grant him strength, healing, comfort, wisdom, and the resilience needed to overcome life's trials and tribulations. Open doors of opportunity that will lead to the restoration of love, prosperity, and happiness in his life.

May you forgive any wrongs committed by this exceptional individual and shower him with abundant blessings. Bestow upon him favor in the eyes of others and imbue him with the courage to face every challenge that comes his way.

If he has lost love, guide him toward its rediscovery. If he seeks financial success, illuminate the path to financial independence. If he battles depression or struggles to find joy in life, reveal to him his intrinsic value and purpose.

For those roles he holds dear, whether as a father or husband, bless him abundantly. Help him embody qualities of understanding, compassion, humility, and courage in his leadership within his family. Grant him the wisdom and strength to be a shining example to his children and a source of pride for his wife.

Grant him the power to overcome every past, present, and future trial. In the name of Jesus, I pray. Amen.

(Prayer for her)

Heavenly Father,

I come before you to lift up this remarkable woman in prayer. Strengthen her spirit and grant her the desires of her heart. Help her recognize her importance within her community, business, family, and relationships. May she find favor with those who can contribute to her satisfaction, peace, and contentment.

Remind her of her inherent value and worth as a queen in your eyes. Grant her the resilience to face and conquer any obstacles hindering her path to restoring love, prosperity, success, and health. If she lacks clarity of vision, bestow upon her a clear purpose and direction. If she carries the burden of heartache, grant her healing and peace in abundance.

I rebuke any presence of depression, poverty, illness, or discontentment in her life. Instead, infuse her with the wisdom and discernment needed to pursue lasting joy and fulfillment. Empower her to lead with grace and integrity in all aspects of her life. Guide her toward fulfilling her destiny as a leader, caretaker, mother, or wife.

For those who depend on her, whether as children or as a spouse, grant her the strength, understanding, and unconditional love to nurture and support them. Grant her the ability to communicate effectively, provide wise direction, and shower them with boundless love.

Forgive her for any mistakes of the past, present, or future, and equip her with the knowledge to grow spiritually, mentally, financially, and physically. Surround her with your divine protection as she courageously forges ahead in her journey. In the name of Jesus, I pray. Amen.

Thank You

"The only people with whom you should try to get

even are those who have helped you."

-John E. Southard

I thank God, the all-powerful, for blessing me with the many challenges I've faced and for giving me the strength and wisdom to overcome them. Without His guidance, I could have been overwhelmed by the difficulties I encountered. I remain dedicated to serving Him always.

I express my gratitude to my beloved wife, Kimberly Thomas, and my wonderful son, Ellard Thomas II. Your unwavering love and support inspire me to persevere. My affection for both of you knows no bounds. You instill in me the belief that I can accomplish anything.

I express gratitude to my father, Terence Taylor, and my late mother, Vanessa Hunter. Your gift of life has afforded me the chance to inspire countless individuals to greatness.

I thank my brothers and sisters: Chris "Vamp" Hunter, Eddie "Deano" Hunter, Shameka "Meka" Williams, and Betty "Missy" Hunter. Each of you embodies greatness. Your boundless love and unwavering support will always be cherished. Keep striving for excellence and achieving your dreams.

I express my deep appreciation to my spiritual mentors, Pastor Gary Hay, Sr., and Dr. Kevin A. Williams. Your guidance and support have been pillars of strength during some of the most challenging moments of my life. Your wisdom and insight have illuminated my path and provided solace in times of darkness.

References

Better Health Channel. Tai Chi Health Benefits.
http://www.betterhealth.vic.gov.au/bhcv2/bhcarticles.
nsf/pages/Tai_Chi

The Diving Life Society. Yoga in Daily Life.
http://www.sivanandaonline.org/graphics/sadhana/yog
a/yoga_dailylife.html

New Beginnings. Accomplishing Dreams Requires Balance.

http://hubpages.com/hub/Accomplishing-Dreams-Requires-
Balance

New King James Bible. (2017) The Holy Bible, NKJV. Online.
https://www.biblestudytools.com/nkjv/

King James Bible. (2017). King James Bible
Online. https://www.kingjamesbibleonline.org/ (Origina
l work published 1769)

Stevenson, Robert (1886). *The Strange Case of Dr. Jekyll and
Mr. Hyde*. Library of Congress.
https://www.loc.gov/item/50041978/

Frost, Robert. *The Road Not Taken.* Poetry Foundation

https://www.poetryfoundation.org/poems/44272/the-road-
not-taken

Bhole Prabhu. *The Meaning and Purpose of Yoga.*

http://www.swamij.com/yoga-meaning.htm

Piper, Watty. (1930). Platt & Munk. *The Little Engine that Could.*

Hill, Napoleon. (1937, 2007). *Think and Grow Rich.* *https://apex.oracle.com/pls/apex/lonestar/r/files/static /v13Y/Think-And-Grow-Rich_2011-06.pdf*

Dan Caro. (2024). *From Tragedy to Triumph.*

https://www.toastmasters.org/magazine/articles/from-tragedy-to-triumph

Obama, Barack. (2008). Yes, We Can.

https://www.englishspeecheschannel.com/english-speeches/barack-obama-speech/

Thomas Jefferson, et al, July 4, 1776, Copy of Declaration of Independence. https://www.archives.gov/founding-docs/declaration-transcript

Made in the USA
Middletown, DE
03 May 2025